Andrew : An

D0982787

£ 1·75

COUNTRY TALK

Illustrated by B. S. BIRO, FSIA

COUNTRY
TALK

J. H. B. Peel

ROBERT HALE · LONDON

First published in Great Britain November 1970
Reprinted February 1971

ISBN 0 7091 1770 1

Robert Hale & Company
63 Old Brompton Road
London S.W.7

Printed and bound in Great Britain by
C. Tinling and Co. Ltd, London and Prescot

Contents

All that is worth remembering in life, is the poetry of it.
William Hazlitt

To
Brian Harvey and Maurice Green
of the *Daily Telegraph*
who go fishing

I

Down to Earth

Some topics do not arouse controversy. It is unthinkable, for example, that doctors could ever dispute the facts of anatomy, or that mathematicians could fail to agree on the solution of a quadratic equation. Country life, by contrast, does arouse controversy. Some people dislike the subject; others dislike what they consider to be an inappropriate way of writing about it. Certainly there are naturalists who overstate the cosmic role of a spotted guzzlethroat. Certainly there are townsfolk who utter ecstatic nonsense about sunsets. Indeed, country life itself has fallen under suspicion; and to write about it at all is akin to spreading false rumours, at any rate in the opinion of some critics.

We may dismiss, as victims of education, the people who speak of 'nature poets' and 'regional novelists' as though the earth, man's *alpha* and *omega*, were an outmoded theatrical scenery. But what are we to make of Quiller-Couch, a sage as rural as the soil, who held that naturalists, having recorded their observations, "ought to be content with communicating them to their fellow-scientists, simply as facts illustrating the infinite and curious work of God". How strange, that a man should be blind to his own wisdom; for if "the infinite and curious" do not arouse wonder, what else can? And if from wonder no poetry flows, whence cometh that "curious" commodity? Those questions seem worth examining.

Most people enjoy a day in the country, but it is only the few to whom Nature—the trees, the birds, the clouds—are something more than an agreeable background. Richard Jefferies expressed the matter very poignantly: "No one else", he sighed, "seems to have seen the sparkle at the brook, or heard the music at the hatch, or to have felt back through the centuries. No one seems to understand how I get food from the clouds, and, when I try to describe these things to them, they stare at me with stolid incredulity." Many people do not share and cannot easily imagine Jefferies' communion with the countryside. To them he appears a figure of fun. Yet if a writer is to do more than pass the time of day, he must on occasion speak the language Jefferies spoke, albeit differently because in his own tone of voice.

What, then, is the nature of the intense delight in country things that has been experienced by many sorts of people—St Francis, Traherne, Wordsworth, Whitman, Mary Webb? Rival psychologies offer their own analyses, and some of them seem valid so far as they venture. Rivers may indeed be symbols of oblivion, and cuckoos the heralds of bastardy. But even when you have traced all guilt to Oedipus, you still have not explained why Oedipus felt guilty. In any event, a man cannot live as though he were permanently on the analyst's couch; nor can psychotherapy relieve him of his need to be a human being. If he feels a chronic aversion from thatched cottages, then he will rightly suppose that there is something amiss in him; but when he gazes enraptured at the curves of a hill, and then goes quietly about his business, he needs not regard himself as a victim of unsatisfactory weaning. A too intensive study of the psychic map may mislead by suggesting unsuitable routes and impossible destinations.

A less technical account of the matter might proceed as follows: to some people the sights, scents, sounds, and colours of the countryside are a sufficient *raison d'être*, exerting an influence so profound that to be divorced from it is intolerable. Everyone knows that Emily Bronte half-killed herself by trying to live away from the Yorkshire Moors. "Day by day," wrote Charlotte, "I watched her sinking, a captive of captivity."

It is not easy to understand any of the mystics; to admire all of them unreservedly is impossible. Nevertheless, their writings show that they have explored levels of consciousness beyond the range of mechanised man. Those levels may be dismissed as deceptive and therefore harmful, but their psychic reality cannot be denied. Nature, however, does not solve the problem of suffering. Nature illustrates it and paints also the 'problem' of joy and co-operation among creatures, without which life would be neither liveable nor worth living. All mystics discover a benign purpose at the heart of things, and some share the Revelation of St John: "God shall wipe away all their tears; and there shall be no more death, neither sorrow nor crying, neither shall there be any more pain: for the former things are passed away." Mysticism never has been a monopoly of bookworms. Wordsworth did not excel at Cambridge, and Beethoven was a very ignorant man. Each in his day endured the reflex response of non-understanding, which is derision. Each was dubbed escapist, sentimentalist, romantic; and it is difficult to say who mocked the louder—the illiterate masses or the cultured mob. Even so, both men were rooted in the soil. From the depth of his deafness Beethoven cried: "When all else fails, there is always the countryside." And from the summit of his fells Wordsworth transcended a logical analysis of the meaning of meaning:

> Wisdom and Spirit of the universe!
> Thou Soul that art eternity of thought. . . .

Calvin was barking up the right tree, but at the wrong twig, when he preached predestination. It may be that some men are genetically doomed to regard the countryside simply as a pretty picture, from which nothing metaphysical can be deduced nor inferred. Many intellectuals certainly practise what J. W. N. Sullivan called "the pleasing but puerile pastime of constructing a philosophy out of the accidents of grammar". Not so the great poets; not so the legion of mute Miltons and village Hampdens; for all were content to abide the question that was put to Job: "Where wast thou when I laid the foundations of the earth? Declare, if thou hast understanding."

Those things can be apprehended, but not comprehended. They are what the lawyers call *ultra vires*. To brood upon them overlong is to paralyse the will and so to flout St Benedict's maxim that work is also worship. It was a Wiltshire parson, George Herbert, who said:

> Who sweeps a room, as for thy laws,
> Makes that and the action fine.

The average countryman, being no fool, does not reject the mystics. He accepts them *cum grano* according to the perceptivity of his palate, for he knows that his own domain lies at the foot-hills of mystery and that the heights above it are profound.

Snowlight and Starlight

I have never been able to decide which is the more enchanting—to watch the first snowflake fall or to awake in a world that went white overnight. Either way, the year's first snow receives a warm welcome, except from those adults who are so grown-up that memory has obliterated their self-portrait of the artist as a young man.

Snow is the most vivid of all the yardsticks by which we measure the variety of our climate. When January brings a few flakes to the South Devon coast, the people there speak of a 'blizzard'. Yet up in Perthshire a fortnight's drifting is accepted with less comment than you hear from Londoners sloshing through an inch of slush.

Snow's visual artistry tends to overshadow its power of silence. The other morning, for example, I walked downhill through the woods to the village, and when I arrived the stillness was audible. People seemed to speak in whispers; their footsteps sounded each alike; no tip-tap of a high-heeled Miss, no rasp of the farmhand's blakeys. The quietness reminded one veteran of his childhood: "In them years you could holler from one end o' the village t'other, and you had to be careful wart you said 'cause wartever you did say, it come bark on you like the bread upon the water. And not after many days it didn't. A couple o' seconds and you heard yourself shouting 'Th'old schoolmaster's barmy'. And by golly if he heard, you was barmy too . . . across your barksoide. There warn't no sissyological methods in them days. No one never spared me on account o' the rod. Reckon thart's why I aren't never been one o' these what-do-you-call-em . . . Ippy boys." And so he went on, a parrot of biased common sense, timeless despite the atomic stop-watch.

Two grooves ran through the village street, carved by a tractor, but only the Royal Mail had dared to follow them. Dethroned from his *hubris*, the pride of ingenuity, man moved as in a humbler age, on foot or astride a horse. Yet he gave thanks for the best of technology, knowing that few people would suffer because help could not reach them. A helicopter or the stalwart ambulance would get through; and if even they failed, still the old craftiness might succeed. I know a district nurse who was able to ease a difficult childbirth at a mountain farm because the blacksmith had towed her thither in a horse-drawn sledge.

Snow plays many variations on the theme of whiteness. There is blinding snow, whipped to a frenzy by the gale. I have encountered it on Exmoor when it blotted out the windscreen and

everything beyond. The lane was already thick with last night's drifting, and I had just time enough to find a gate and there put-about for home before every ditch and dyke became invisible. Travelling at twelve miles an hour, with my head out of the window, I watched the lane disappear beneath a general conformity.

There is dazzling snow, as at noon on a cloudless sky, when the glare hurts the eyes, and every furrow wears a pink sheen, and all windowpanes blaze brighter than headlamps at midnight. The Swiss, who are accustomed to such brilliance, wear dark glasses, but the English associate snow with Robert Southey's sombre landscape:

> Blue-lipt, an ice-drop at thy sharp blue nose,
> Plodding alone through sleet and drifting snows.

There is fantastic snow, which appears when frost follows a blizzard. Emerson called it "frolic architecture". Plump cliffs overhang from hedges, as though a pastrycook had passed by, icing a mile-long cake. Trees mime penguins. The ugly bungalow resembles a thatched cottage that has subsided, and now reveals only the dormers peering like blue eyes beneath white eyebrows.

And there is snow by starlight, callous as one whose physical beauty knows no moral law. Birds die without falling, frozen to their perch. Trees are spliced as though by an axe. All lanes become a skating rink, and each footstep through the field sounds like a broken window. Out of doors one tries to keep warm, but never wholly succeeds. Sawing logs, a cottager wipes the sweat from his forehead, with hands too cold to feel it.

All those variations end where they began, on a note of beauty and astonishment. Even the commonest objects achieve a new nobility. The lid of the dustbin ceases to be a lump of cheap metal, and becomes a marble crown, an emblem of chivalry, art's rebuke to the conscious representation of a non-representational Unconscious. The woods are a gloss on reality; no Christmas card ever excelled their blend of chasteness and baroque; no palette outshone the variety of their black-and-whiteness. Shelley declared:

> I love snow, and all forms
> Of the radiant frost. . . .

Coventry Patmore was less singular than he supposed:

> I, singularly moved
> To love the lovely that are not beloved,
> Of all the Seasons, most
> Love Winter. . . .

If you are hale, and have no need to travel, the snowclad countryside weaves a spell; and the further you look, the more you are spellbound. Vehicles abandoned overnight suggest the shape of things that came and then went a million years ago. Climbing a bare skyline, the grooves of a tractor lead the imagina-

tion backward through the centuries, to a time when the world
was younger, and men explored it, and in all the steppes there
was but one road, made by one man who might—and might not—
have survived what he had found in the deep and startled valley.
Highbanked lanes reveal Praxiteles working alongside Michel-
angelo in a realm of alabaster. Lovely, too, is the little railway
station with its castellated Victoriana frozen into stalactites, and
the black rails curving like a question-mark through fairyland.

The House on a Hill

Having wandered through woods for several miles, the lane
suddenly came into the open, and I found myself on an escarp-
ment of the Chilterns, a country so familiar to me that I felt
chastened as well as surprised when, in a nearby copse, I saw the
roof of a cottage which I had never before noticed. And then I
went on, idly wondering who it was that lived amid such splendid
isolation.

Walking downhill, I perceived the full splendour of that isolation. Ahead, on the skyline, Wittenham Clumps resembled a
walled city in a treeless world; below, vast hedgeless fields heaved
and then subsided; behind, the beechwoods shone like besoms on
a brown carpet. Here indeed were height and depth, and things
pastoral and things arable, all leavened with that blend of intimacy
and spaciousness which only the Chiltern by-lanes offer. Suddenly I halted, and went back, led by curiosity to discover who
kept house in what appeared to be

> A land where no man comes,
> Nor hath come since the making of the world.

As I say, the cottage stood in a copse, along a grass path,
secluded even from the unfrequented lane. At fifty yards I could
see that the place was empty; after twenty yards I guessed that it
was derelict; and when I reached the door I decided that the decay
had set in long ago. Parts of the cottage were very old—the
timbers said so—and some of the bricks still glowed with a
healthy tan; but the window frames seemed to have been tacked-
on as an afterthought, and I was able to thrust a finger between

B

the wood and the wall. Traces of what had evidently been a well-kept garden were visible under a wilderness of weeds.

I turned again to the cottage; two up and two down, I thought. If the trees were lopped a little, the upper windows would enjoy one of the three finest views in Oxfordshire (the second being from Christmas Common). I found myself torn between sorrow (that a home had been allowed to disintegrate) and fantasy (that I might buy it and the view that went therewith). Where, I wondered, was the nearest shop? A moment's thought replied: the nearest shop was also the only shop, in an off-beat hamlet far below and out of sight.

Again I looked at the cottage. There were no wires of any kind, so the place certainly lacked a telephone. But what if I had a heart attack at three o'clock on a snowbound morning? And then, again, what if I did not? The man who plans for his own decrepitude has already reached it. Even so, I winced at the thought of what it would cost to make the house habitable. Forty years ago I could have bought it for one hundred pounds. Now they would charge that for decorating a couple of rooms.

I stooped to peer through a window; and next moment I jumped several inches into the air, stung by an invisible voice.

"Wart you warnt?"

"I'm terribly sorry. I'd no idea. I. . . ."

"You a London gent? No, oi didn't think you was. You got a good colour you 'ave. Don't reckon you'll fall down dead. Not this year anyway."

"But . . . is the place occupied?"

" 'Tis when I'm in it."

Dammit, I thought, some old tramp; but I was wrong. The tumbledown idyll really was occupied, and presently the occupant appeared, a neat-looking man, slightly deaf. We began to talk.

"Oi was born 'ere. And thart's sixty-five year ago. Oi aren't never bin anywhere else 'cept 'ospital. Went to school down in the village. And thart's a long way, in case you didn't know. Ah, and it gits longer when you come bark 'cause it's upill. It's all 'ills 'ere."

He tapped his pipe before deigning to acknowledge my facetious inquiry.

"No, oi aren't got a telly. There's enough to think about without looking at one o' them damned things. Who? No, oi aren't married neither. Oi got a niece. She drops in now and again for my washing. Ah, and oi got a nephew-in-law as you might say. He brings groceries. Paint?" He looked at the peeling window-frames. " 'Tis a bit thin, yes, but there is *some* 'cause I done it my-self. Anyow, it's a small rent."

"Did you never try to buy the place?"

"Oi troid. Thirty year ago oi troid, when things was a sight cheaper nor wart they are now. But they wouldn't sell. They didn't warnt to, they said. Mind you, the landlord's a nice enough charp. Always looks in, round about rent toime, t'ask if th'old roof leaks."

"Does it?"

"Not yet. How do oi wart? Oi don't. There's no lavatory, no 'lectric, no 'phone, no water."

"No water? How on earth do you manage?"

"Rain bucket."

"But what happens when the bucket's empty?"

"Oi goes and fills it. Where? Why, the nearest farm, o' course. Thart's upill. It's always the same in these parts. If a thing isn't on the top, it's roight down the bottom. Good for the 'ealth, oi suppose. Oh ah, it's quiet all roight. But who warnts noise?"

"Have you always been on your own?"

"No. My old mother lived 'ere, too, and thart warnt all them years ago. Garden? No, oi can't do wart oi used. Oi 'ad it lovely one toime, but then oi said, you gotta give up one day, oi said, so why not today? And oi did."

For a third time I glanced at the damp, decaying cottage, and was so shocked that I said: "I wonder they haven't condemned it."

"Condemned?" He looked up sharply, as though after all I might be a London gent. "Oi aren't agoing to git myself dragged into thart line o' talk. You got to be careful wart you say nowa-days. T'ain't like th'old toimes when you could call a fella a liar and all he did was call you a bloody bigger one. But oi don't worry. Like wart oi said, oi got a niece. Oi reckon she won't let me go downhill not without she puts a bit o' grease on the road so's t'ease the way loike. Oh ah, you come bark one day and 'ave another chart."

Stuck in the Mud

There are not many dispiriting days in winter. Rivers may freeze, and snow will fall, but a thaw arrives next week—except perhaps in the mountains, where they are accustomed to such delays. Even so, dull days do dawn, and then a countryman either sits by the fire or goes out to make the best of what he can find. Sometimes he cannot find anything at all until he has bumped into it, for this is the weather when the sun rises and sets invisibly. Cattle graze ten yards beyond the window, and they too are out of sight, swathed in a smoke-screen of their own making. To walk becomes simply a physical act, the exercise of prisoners around a yard. The trees seem to have marched from Macbeth's fateful Dunsinane; instead of staying rooted, they advance on you, spikey as a Breughel winter, each twig dripping like a nose.

Sounds, too, deceive the senses; even keen senses and even on their home ground. Walking the cliff path toward Lynton, I went warily, waiting for the sea to remind me that I had reached a point which invites caution. But there was neither sound nor sight of the sea, though I knew that it lay eight hundred feet below. I therefore turned back, not on my own account but because of the dog, which was somewhere on the port bow and very much off the beaten track. Fumbling through nether-night, I uttered the prayer which Francis Quarles sent up to Phosphor or Venus:

> bring the day
> Whose conquering ray
> May chase these fogs, sweet Phosphor, bring the day.

Dry coldness stops short of warm wool, but not even an oilskin offers much comfort against raw weather. You can stride through crisp snow and then halt without losing temperature; in a mist you seem always to sweat and never to glow. Arthur Clough hoped that our endeavours are not ultimately futile— "Say not the struggle naught availeth"—but what hope is there for the man who goes walking in a mist? The fields (which he cannot see) and the waves (which he does not hear) mock his muscles. He is pitting himself against a climate which lacks all

22.50

Luup B S

1979

Sunday

~~June~~ 3rd

Arrival Day

1st Field Day

Wed.

June 20 th

Ideal Girl

Friday

July 6 th

merit, and therefore invites no praise. He were better at home, buttering toast before the fire, sipping with William Cowper

> the cups that cheer,
> But not inebriate. . . .

January—the summit of winter—persuades us that these dank days occur often. But they do not. They are rarities despite the cynic who keeps no journal, and relies solely on a jaundiced memory. Coleridge preached wisely when he said: "Therefore all seasons shall be dear to thee." Like every other mortal, Coleridge was not always able to practise his own sermons. When winter had fouled the Quantock lanes, he anathematized them as "Confusion's quagmire". Mud is indeed an unedifying aspect of country ways in winter. Clay or chalk, the stuff clings to your boots, and walks home with you. Housewives call from kitchens: "Don't keep walking in and out like that. Just look at the mess you've made!"

Re-entry into the house becomes a ritual. First, you remove one boot at the back door; then you set a stockinged foot on the news-papered floor, hoping to discard the other boot while you balance half in and half out of the kitchen. Alas, even the best newsprint inclines to slither, and then you must choose between plonking a muddy boot in the kitchen or a stockinged sole on the concrete. Attempting the former, you sometimes achieve the latter.

Many of our by-ways are as muddy as when Llewelyn Powys remembered them eighty years ago: "The country lanes were foul," he complained, "and the road from the vicarage to the church ran with two streams of rain-water, the Thames and the Severn as we children called them." In the grip of such ruts you chide Vergil because he wrote *fortunas* instead of *mucus*: "O muddy countrymen!" Yet mud, after all, is but another name for earth, mingled with water, whereof we are ourselves composed. I doubt that a dose of pure mud ever harmed anyone. As we say: "It'll brush off when it's dry."

If you do plunge into the chiaroscuro, you find a cross-section of the calendar. You find April's beechleaves, bound tight as a copper cartridge. You find September's blackberry, withered away to near-nothingness. You find December's holly and the catkins of March. You find a June rose, lone as an aged man who has outlived his children's children. You find trees so bare that even their bark looks thin; and others still flaunting a halo of gingery leaf. And you find derelict birdnests that touch the heart because they remind you of human homes and of the domestic joy and sorrow that are life itself.

January sifts the true countrymen from the fairweather visitors; for whereas the latter will abhor brash wind and squelching mud, the former are well-pleased to breathe the open air, perceiving beauty where others detect only decay. Nevertheless, the dark days seem interminable, and night's curtain falls as it were on a modern play whose purpose is to preach a gospel of loneliness, despair, futility. Fresh air resembles Timothy's wine; if we take a sip, it is solely for the sake of our digestion. Such days plumb the zero of a season which W. H. Davies detested:

> Within whose mist no dewdrops shine,
> And grass, once green, goes yellow;
> For whom no bird will sing or chirp
> From either ash or willow.

Yet the willow and the ash, like the bird and the grass, are retreating in order to advance. Having lately changed its name, the new year will perceptibly lighten our darkness.

Where All Roads Meet

Suddenly you become relaxed and at the same time more alert. The sensation itself is universal, but the precise moment at which it occurs is very private. Some people experience it when they are halfway down a street in Stepney. Other and more fortunate travellers—like a friend of mine who lives in Norfolk—recognise the symptoms when they leave the Newmarket road, and bear left among woods toward Swaffham. Others, again, meet it on the lane from Arkholme to Kirkby Lonsdale, where the fells write Westmorland on the sky. All have reached their own territory.

Home, in short, is more than a house; it is a segment of the spokes which radiate from that house; and the farther we are accustomed to travel, the wider will be our homeland. A limit must be set, of course, else home will come to include every place from which we return. Perhaps we may adopt a sliding scale.

For example, most countryfolk use the word 'home' to describe the fields which they have learned closely by walking or riding across them. Yet even that seems too flexible, for a man in his youth will stride thirty miles, and still feel the better for it. Six miles is a reasonable compromise, an area that will teach us every bend in the road, every stile by the way, all houses, churches, streams, woods, ponds, beaches, mountains, lakes, pubs, signposts, and people. Those are the sedative and also the tonic which, when you do meet them, cause you to become relaxed and at the same time more alert.

James Smeaton—architect of the third Eddystone Light—died at the house in which he was born, having made it his home for sixty-eight years. Few folk nowadays live so firmly rooted; fewer still would wish to do so. Old Fynes Moryson despised such static evolution: "They seem to me most unhappy, and no better than prisoners who, from cradle to old age, still behold the same walls, the same faces, orchards, pastures and objects of the eye." Christopher Harvey held the contrary view: "He that doth live at home, and learns God and himself, needeth no farther go." Maybe a middle way is best, like a boat swinging freely from a sure anchorage.

It is interesting to compare notes on the subject. I knew a sea-captain who was so much a citizen of the world that he felt at home in any quarter of it where the temperature exceeded 70° F. For him, he said, home appeared on the second morning out from Southampton, when the steward prepared his white uniform. Other friends have told me of more precise horizons: a wooded by-way through the Chilterns above Velvet Lawn; or that bend in the road near Tennyson's birthplace on the Lincolnshire wolds, where a signpost points to Ashby Puerorum; or the Exmoor lane looping one-in-three from Martinhoe to Heddon's Mouth; or the mountainous track from Cwman to Maesllan; or the switchback from Braemar to Tomintoul, Scotland's highest village. There are indeed many memorable homecomings. Think of the islander whose island is itself on an island—like the farmer who rows home by moonlight to his bield on a loch. Think of that other farmer, away in Caithness, whose croft lies at the far end of twenty miles of single-track-with-passing-places; *ultima thule* the ancients called his home, "the end of the world". Think of England's loneliest lock-keeper beside the Thames at Shifford in Oxfordshire; his heavy wares arrive by water, but the light ones must be fetched via a towing path and several miles of narrow lane. Think of those forest homes without even a track—only footsteps rustling the silence.

Perhaps you know the land above Tregaron, that wildest part of Cardiganshire. No road crosses those high, inclement solitudes. The old drovers did tread a path into the hills, but their motto was "So far, and then no farther". Only the hardiest emerged on the other side of desolation. Yet you will see a cottage there. No place is so unpromising that the dweller cannot find what Hilaire Belloc discovered on his Sussex Downs:

> Here am I homeward
> from my wandering,
> Here am I homeward
> and my heart is healed.

"Home, Sweet Home" is a simple lyric, set to a simple tune. The sincerity of its attempt to express true love, transcends the mockery of cynics. Home, after all, is our autobiography, indelibly private and perennially universal. To the Romans it was literally an abode of gods or holy spirits. When political enemies had destroyed his own home, Cicero arraigned their sacrilege, in words that must have pierced the heart of all who heard them: "Is there anything else," he cried, "more hallowed, more hedged about with every kind of sanctity, than the home of each individual citizen?" To Ovid a love of home was both "invincible and inexplicable":

> *Nescio qua natale solum dulcedine captos*
> *Ducit. . . .*

Like the birds, each countryman has his territory, and neither a time of year nor the hour of the day will blur his recognition of it. Snow may obliterate the tops of the hedges, but it cannot hide the height of the hills. Clouds may cancel the stars, but sooner or later a tree or a bridge utters the unspoken word. Fog, fatigue, sorrow, joy—a thousand things may cheat the senses or stifle remembrance—yet somewhere along the way our *alter ego*, the friend of many years, comes out to greet us. It is as though, in Pauline phrase, home's old acquaintance will yield to nothing—"neither death, nor life, nor principalities, nor powers, nor things present, nor things to come". Always the light shineth and is seen.

> what, on earth, is half so dear—
> So longed for—as the hearth of home?

Emily Bronte's question is also a description of her native moorland, which she approached via "a little and a lone green lane". But home is more than a lane. It is the place where all roads meet.

A Man of Village Affairs

A country lawyer's office is a mirror of country life: always vivid, often humorous, sometimes tragic. The one I have in mind faces a market cross through windows frosted half-way up. Behind, a walled garden slopes to a stream. Except for some deed boxes and a pile of sale catalogues, the office might have belonged to any bookish man. In it, whenever I visited those parts, I used to seek counsel's opinion on many topics while sipping coffee beside a coal fire with a good companion who has lately retired from earthly litigation.

The solicitor himself was a great rider to hounds. On Wednesdays, they said, he worked for one hour only, booted and spurred for the chase. But he was a scholar, too, fond of reading Vergil when business was slack. Even in private conversation he preferred the Latin word which did the work of three English. As a youth he tried his fortune in London, but soon wearied of the soot, and settled in the village, and flourished there until he died. His father had done precisely the same. Two manslaughterers were defended from the office, as well as a trio who went to prison for relieving the Royal Mint of its duties. However, most of the village misdemeanours were petty—rear lights (or lack of them), Saturday evening insobriety, and man's immemorial habit of breaking a contract. Those, of course, are indoor cases; but our lawyer's work often led him into the open air. He learned to recognise a good crop of hay and the ill-drained meadow. By way of payment in kind he once accepted six Devon Longwools which so pleased him that he rented a meadow, and dabbled at sheep farming. He mastered the law of trespass by walking it. They used to say that he could discuss any footpath or parish boundary for miles around without consulting the map.

Like priests and doctors, a lawyer sees—or at any rate over-hears—the skeleton in village cupboards. For example, the solici-tor once employed a retired policeman to prevent a wealthy spinster from drinking herself to death. Although the policeman scrutinised all callers at the house, and examined the parcel post, several weeks passed before he discovered that the booze was being smuggled by a gardener at night; the spinster hauling it to her window on a string. Strangest of all, it was she who had com-missioned the solicitor to thwart her own ingenuity.

Like his father before him, he handled the legal affairs at the Hall; but times change, and whereas the father in his youth attended as a servant, the son in his age dined above the salt, whence he gleaned many snippets of scandal, politics, and racing. He once said that a dozen good tips, straight from the horse owner's mouth, had enabled him to send his sons to Cambridge.

Mr Bumble dismissed the law as "a ass". But our lawyer was no fool. "Whenever you're passing," he used to say, "drop in for a chat." And because he listened well, his invitation was well received, at a profit to himself of six-and-eightpence. Yet I never heard the cottagers complain that poverty had deprived them of our counsel's opinion. Like Robin Hood, though with more respect for the law, he sometimes took from the rich in order to act for the poor. Twice I heard him defend a motorist in court, and twice his plea prevailed. Had he set his hand to a more ambitious plough, he would have reaped a richer harvest, like Chaucer's fee-fond lawyer who rode in fine clothes to Canterbury:

> Of fees and robes he had many a one,
> So great a purchaser was nowhere known,
> All was fee simple to him. . . .

At one period of his life our solicitor did spend some time in London, researching for a treatise on equity and the conveyance of Fransican property to boroughs, but again the soot unsettled him. He preferred the fields of home, finding there a sufficient renown and an adequate income. I often likened him to the man in Steele's essay: "The sad, the merry, the severe, the melancholy, show a new cheerfulness when he comes amongst them. He does not seem to contribute to the mirth of the company, and yet upon reflection you find that it all happened by his being there."

Our great-grandfathers chuckled when *Punch* declared: "What is the difference between a barrister and a solicitor? Merely the difference between a crocodile and an alligator." Country-folk always have regarded lawyers with distaste, but our lawyer was approved despite his calling. To borrow of his own beloved Latin, he was a blend of Aquinas and Scotus, *angelicus subtilisque*. Grateful for his sympathy and common sense, the villagers revered him as *prudens*, or a wise man, the appellation which Rome bestowed upon her legal experts. Was he then blameless? By no means: some of his opinions on crime and punishment were held against the evidence; and it was significant that he dismissed Freud (whom he had never read) as a licentious quack. Sometimes he gave the impression that the Law Lords combined omniscience with infallibility. In such moods he would refer every kind of dilemma to the precedent of Shirley v Fagg.

Like many of his class and generation, he knew that manners makyth clothes. Except for those pink (and probably apocryphal) Wednesdays, his uniform was a black jacket and striped trousers; out of doors he wore what he called pepper-and-salt. And what a book he might have written, had ethics and his own reticence made it possible. Many of us would still like to know what really did happen when the heir, having sold his estates for eighty thousand pounds, was sued six months later for the price of a topcoat: gambling, we wondered, or blackmail?

The new solicitor is a young man whose broom has already dispersed several relics. The friendly fireside is now an impersonal electric stove; the pink tape has been replaced by elastic bands; and instead of ringing a silver bell, he summons his clerk by house-telephone. But humanity itself cannot be brushed aside so easily. On my last visit I was assured that the new village counsellor is still much concerned with disputed boundaries, defective headlamps, and the youth who changed his mind before the wedding.

2

The First Signs of Spring

When does spring arrive? The calendar says, "In March." But February will sometimes whisper, "Now." And the whisper comes soonest and softest in the far south-west, where I have a hilltop house, near a point where Exmoor greets the coast of Devon.

Science has made nonsense of many of the old calendars. Nowadays you can buy anemones on New Year's Eve; and the lambs in winter are dropped as lightly as snowflakes. Even so, one must attempt some sort of definition of spring, else the word will grow meaningless by being used of any mild morning. Spring, surely, is the sum of specific and observable events, among which I would include the first daffodil and the last crocus. It is an eventful season; and on Exmoor lately many things have been happening. This morning, for example, a blackbird came to drink at the stream. Suddenly—as though it had remembered that the stream itself sings throughout the year—the bird let loose those notes I had not heard since September. Sir William Beach Thomas told the whole truth and nothing more when he said: "Bird-song can make a very real difference to life." Nor did Meredith overstate the fact that the year's first song is unforgettable:

> His Island voice then you shall hear,
> Nor ever after separate
> From such a twilight of the year,
> Advancing to the vernal gate.

Unlike temperature, birdsong is a reliable chronometer. To some people, indeed, the first sounds of spring are more welcome even than the first sights; and the gladdest sound of all comes from the "bare ruin'd choirs" where once again the sweet birds sing.

The house, by the way, is only a short distance from the sea, along a path through a ravine whose summits are invisible unless you crick your neck to look up at them. After ten minutes' walk a timber footbridge carries you over the stream, and two more minutes bring you to a small beach that remains your own through nine of the twelve months. There, the other afternoon, spring stepped ashore, followed by wavelets playful as a puppy. The rocks were warm to lean against. For the first time since September the sun was so searching that you could not easily look it in the face. Larks walked the plank of a cliff, and then checked their fall, soaring out of sight though never beyond the sound of their song. Six hundred years ago Dafydd ap Gwilym saw the same thing in Wales: "Under your beating wings," he wrote, "is the miraculous grace of God, carrying you up to those heights." Nor is our welcome reserved for the mastersingers; we greet the rooks also, whose harsh music reminds us that the birds haunted their old home throughout the winter, as though to deter squatters among the "immemorial elms". Joseph Addison admired rooks despite and yet because of their guttural chatter: "I am very much delighted with this Sort of Noise, which I consider as a kind of natural Prayer to that Being who supplies the Wants of his whole Creation, and who, in the beautiful Language of the Psalms, feedeth the young Ravens that call upon him."

White as the gulls, an intrepid yacht has launched herself on this breath of spring. From the Roman signal station above Martinhoe I watch her graceful progress, borne forward by a following wind . . . not Shelley's "wild, west wind", but a spur that swells the sails, and with its rowel carves both wake and bow-wave. Then, abeam of Lynmouth, she disappears, having as it were signalled that she had sighted the halcyon days.

Inland, along a lane through the heart of the moor, men are sweeping the grit that will be used against next winter's blizzard. On the hotel lawn a lad re-paints deck chairs, ready for Easter. At this hour a month ago the farmer's wife was lighting the oil lamps; now she is in the garden, transplanting her wallflowers.

At first sight the countryside in February seems much as it did in December, but second thoughts detect the changes. Rooks are repairing last year's nest. Young wheat glows like greensward.

The scar on the twig is a bud. Ewes approach their time, and the catkins are indeed 'lambs' tails'. Richard Jefferies said that insects were "the makers of summer" . . . the bees and the butterflies feeding from flower to flower. The makers of spring are these measurable moments that now invite us to stroll after tea through a sunset whose flowers, like Mallarmé, pay their own devoir to the spring:

> Tout en moi s'exaltait de voir
> La famille des iridées
> Surgir à ce houvease devoir.

So, while our friends up in Westmorland were chucking another log on the fire, the dog and I strolled in the sunshine, splashing through Tarr Steps, hearing the wavelets at Heddon's Mouth, watching the deer on Robin How. And in the tap room at nightfall the postman praised his precocious vegetables: "My dear soul, they'm springing up quicker than grandchildren." Winter, in short, had broken its back, though not until men were staggering beneath the last snow-flecked straw.

In the country, where foxes abound, we do not count our chickens until we have trussed them; so with the seasons also. March winds and April showers wait ahead. May itself has been known to shiver. But when the February sun does shine, and the breakers become ripples, then at last a countryman knows that he will soon be justified in reciting the loveliest of all greetings to spring: "For, lo, the winter is past, the rain is over and gone; the flowers appear on the earth; the time of the singing of birds is come, and the voice of the turtle is heard in our land."

A Village Blacksmith

The old rhyme says:

> Under a spreading chestnut tree
> The village smithy stands.

During his tea-break the smith himself may stand there, but in working hours he is more likely to be found lying under a tractor, goggled and gaseous, while he welds the fracture.

Why does a village blacksmith stir the imagination? Why do

villagers and visitors collect around his anvil, as moths beseige a flame? Is it because our mechanised era responds to the skill of one-man capitalism? Is it because the smith stands—or is assumed to stand—in danger of extinction? An answer to those questions does not demand a retreat into prehistory, but it does invite a brief glance backward. During the 1920s a new sort of horse-

power began to rule the roads, and the old sort disappeared. As a result, the smiths seemed likely to join the dodo because many of them could not, or would not, adapt their ancient skills to modern tasks. The number of blacksmiths continues to decrease, and so does the number of horses. We have no official census, but in 1970 the Clerk to the Farriers' Company put the number of British horses at about 200,000, of which 30,000 were racehorses. Yet a considerable number of village smiths continue to earn a living. Why? There are two basic reasons.

First, the smith has adapted himself to a changed environment, often with help from the Rural Industries Bureau. I could name a dozen elderly men who were taught the latest methods of welding. Previously they had not known how to make the best use of their equipment, and were losing both time and money by jotting their accounts onto scraps of paper. The second reason for the smiths' solvency is the multiplication of farm machines, which has partly offset the decline in shoeing. Tractors and combines do not need to be shod regularly, but their maintenance and repair cost very much more than a new set of shoes.

The blacksmith whom I know best is Jonty Wilson of Kirkby Lonsdale in Westmorland. Shoeing represents only a small fraction of his income, and would be even less were it not that he tends a stud on a local estate. Every day he repairs farm implements—spades, rakes, tines, posts, gates—and every week he repairs farm machines. His forge is permanently littered with lawn-mowers, bicycles, and kitchen utensils which he will mend as a farmer mends his hedges—when, and if, he finds time to do so. Several Westmorland churches and houses display the weather vanes and iron gates that were commissioned from him.

When Jonty Wilson became a blacksmith's apprentice sixty-five years ago he received half-a-crown a week during the first three years, and thereafter five shillings until he came of age. As a craftsman, with wife and children to support, he received £64 a year. In his early days a blacksmith's labour cost the customer sixpence an hour; many village smiths now charge a guinea an hour. Which came first: the increased wage or the rising cost? In 1913, for example, Jonty Wilson bought his iron at £5 a ton; in 1920 he paid £20 for it; in 1970 he paid £80. During the past half-century the price of his fuel has risen by 400 per cent. In 1913 a set of light shoes cost half-a-crown; in 1920, eleven shillings; in 1970, nearly £2.

It is not by chance that Smith remains the commonest name in a telephone directory. Even in Scotland it remains the commonest, outnumbering MacGregor and MacDonald. Place-names, too, testify to the blacksmith's former importance. Hammersmith is perhaps the best-known example. Others include Smeeth in Yorkshire, Smeetham Hall in Essex, Smeeton Westerby in

Leicestershire, Smethwick in Staffordshire, Smethcote in Shropshire, Smisby in Derbyshire (London's Smithfield, however, was the *smethe feld* or smooth field). Inns, also, recall departed glories: the Plough and Harrow (a smith's handiwork), the Blacksmith's Arms, and the Three Horseshoes, part of the arms of the Farriers' Company, showing two horses supporting "argent, three horseshoes sable, pierced of the field", above the motto *Vi et Virtute* or, in the vernacular, Brawn and Integrity.

Farriers had their own fraternity six centuries ago. Their present spokesman is the Worshipful Company of Farriers, which received a charter from King Charles II so that it might improve the standard of workmanship, and apprehend "every misdemeanour and defective workes and medicines to the intent that due and legall prosecution may be had and taken against all and every such offenders". Two centuries later, in 1890, the Company instituted the examination and registration of shoeing smiths; and in 1923 the village smith became eligible for fellowship of the Company. More than ten thousand smiths have passed the various grades of examination. The Company's freemen have included a Duke and a Field-Marshal.

Britain is littered with obsolete forges. Near Sweetheart Abbey in Scotland the old forge is now a private residence; at Seathwaite in Lancashire it is a disused barn; at Gerrans in Cornwall it became part of a tea shop. But not all is Ichabod. At the foot of the lane to Little Hampden in Buckinghamshire the forge was closed during the 1930s, and remained empty for decades. Now it has re-opened to ply a brisk trade among mechanised farmers and social-status-riding-folk.

From time immemorial the village smithy has been the men's gossip place. Indeed, Anglo-Saxon law allowed that anything uttered within the smithy should enjoy the kind of immunity which we now bestow on Members of Parliament. The smithy has changed since I first knew it, more than fifty years ago. Then, on a winter's evening, the old men huddled on the bench before a fire that was the only light; gossiping, smoking, spitting, musing. Today the smithy has electricity and a telephone. Yet some old things abide: the music on the anvil, the shower of sparks therefrom, a horse patiently untroubled by its acrid hoof-smoke, and—among the old men's ageing sons—the same immortal talk of crops, weather, time-passing, and the price of beer.

A Day to Remember

Hell, they say, is full good intentions; and in February our diary begins to look empty of them. Yet how conscientiously we started the new year, entering Auntie's birthday, a date *à deux* (with the dentist), and on the appropriate page the number of our season ticket, date of expiry of driving licence, size in collars, and whatever other intimacies we felt might interest whatever other audience we had in mind—the coroner, perhaps, or (in the event of our becoming Unexpectedly Famous) some avid Boswell. And now, so few weeks later, the pages, like Cassius, look dangerously lean. If we are honest we confess ourselves weary of writing: "Had the new neighbours in for drinks. Shan't again." . . . "Am dreadfully worried about C. Feel certain his fiancée is unsuitable." . . . "Uncle called while the wife was washing her hair." . . . "Today is my eighteenth birthday and have achieved *nothing*." We conclude our denigration with a rhetorical question: "Anyway, who on earth cares *what* I do or think?"

But softly: "There must," said Robert Bridges, "be thousands and thousands of persons alive at this very moment in England, who, if only they could give expression to those mysterious feelings with which they are moved in the presence of natural beauty, would be one and all of them greater poets than have ever yet been." Before he became Poet Laureate, Bridges had practised as a doctor in a semi-slum, and was therefore unlikely to exaggerate the artistic potential of ordinary men and women. Let us, however, omit the 'if only' and 'poetic expression'. Let us take the Laureate's profound truth at one-half of its face value, by rephrasing it: "There must be thousands and thousands of persons alive at this very moment in England (and in Scotland and Wales and Ulster), who, if only they kept a different sort of diary, could give immense pleasure to themselves and perhaps to other people also." For example, on 22nd September 1880 Henri Amiel wrote in his own diary: "When I opened my eyes this morning I saw the sun in a clear sky. It is now 11 a.m. and for the last four hours I have been bathed in its radiance, exercising all my senses with delight—seeing, hearing, smelling, breathing." There follows another simple entry: "I have been sauntering along familiar paths through the countryside to look once more on the lake, the hills, the orchards. . . ."

Or consider this: "One of my neighbours, an intelligent and observing man, informs that, in the beginning of May, about ten minutes before eight o'clock in the evening, he discovered a great cluster of house-swallows, thirty at least he supposes, perching on a willow on the verge of James Knight's upper-pond." That entry was made by a country parson, Gilbert White, in his *Natural History of Selborne.*

Or consider this, by another country parson, James Woodforde, who in February 1779 wrote: "Never known such fine weather at this season of the year, and of so long continuance ever since the storm of Jan 1st. It was like June today. Thanks to God for such glorious weather."

Or consider this, from the journal of a not-so-young spinster, written between intervals of cooking and darning; to wit, Dorothy, sister of the poet Wordsworth: "I never saw daffodils so beautiful. They grew among the mossy stones about and about them; some rested their heads upon these stones as on a pillow for weariness; and the rest tossed and reeled and danced, and seemed as if they verily laughed with the wind . . . they looked so gay, so glancing, ever changing."

Some days later, inspired because reminded by Dorothy's journal, Wordsworth composed one of the best-loved poems in our language:

> I wandered lonely as a cloud
> That floats on high o'er vales and hills,
> When all at once I saw a crowd,
> A host, of golden daffodils;
> Beside the lake, beneath the trees,
> Fluttering and dancing in the breeze.

Or consider this, by Mary Webb: "I have gone to see the white clover fall asleep in the meadows. Kneeling and looking very close, as the dew begins to gather, one sees a slight change in the leaves; all round, the green is paler than by day when the dark upper surfaces of the leaves are beneath the flowers." And to that exact observation she adds a wider vision: "We see nature red in tooth and claw, and so it is; but it is so much else as well; it is dewy, it is honey-sweet, it is full of the soft voices of young creatures and the reassuring tones of motherhood."

Most people will agree that those entries are both informative and beautiful; yet none was written in a style beyond the reach of readers who care for such things; and all are such things as may be seen from any lane and from many gardens in a town. The secret (if it be a secret) is to look closely, to listen intently, and then to describe briefly the sounds and sights, the people and places, which seem the most pleasing, or most puzzling, or most challenging.

February seems an excellent time to start a journal of one's own, for the earth has stirred from an apparent sleep, and her movement will soon unfold the snowdrop. Defying any parental *contre-temps* they may have overheard in their own nestling days, the birds are courting again, which is to say kissing and quarrelling and generally playing the fool whom wise men frown on. And when the birds have hatched their first brood, out will come the first leaf, like a sentry with a sunshade.

There is no need for the diarist to perpetrate purple prose nor to ferret after recondite facts. Woodforde's journal began with an entry wherein brevity dead-heated with banality: "We lodged at the King's Arms in Evershot, where we had exceeding good Port Wine." Yet that *Diary of a Country Parson* became a classic. Even although you are the only reader of your journal, and have yet to tell the difference between cabbage and kale, still you will be engrossed while you watch, tested while you write, and rewarded when you have written. Who knows, somebody may pay you the supreme compliment which Wordsworth offered to his sister, with one omniscient line:

> She gave me eyes, she gave me ears.

Beating About the Bush

There are times when a countryman inclines to believe that the farmhands have hibernated. You can travel a hundred miles without seeing anyone at work on the land. Inwardly, of course, you know very well that the cows are being milked, the sheep fed, the drains laid, the gates mended, and countless letters dispatched to inquisitive auditors and incredulous Ministries. Yet still the fields seem empty of men, as though men themselves were mere sleeping partners in a concern that went its own way unattended. If you do notice someone at work, he will probably be layering a hedge. "How neat," exclaims the townsman, meaning: "How nice of the farmer to provide such a pleasing ornament." And the townsman may add: "All the same, it seems rather a laborious way of marking the boundaries."

Hedges do indeed mark boundaries, but that is neither their chief nor their sole function. A hedge serves as a windbreak for crops and as a nesting-place for birds. That cattle also find shelter

is (so to say) a by-product and no kindly forethought by farmers, some of whom treat their stock in a way which is best described as heartless: thumping, lashing, cursing. Our dumb friends never were mute, and may at times appear downright hostile, but that does not entitle us to hurt them.

As for layering a hedge, there is no mystery about it; nothing of the uncanny psychic power which makes a good shepherd worth more than his wages. Hedging requires only deftness and common sense. Like every other skill, it improves with practice. I am rather clumsy at it myself, having seldom attempted it since my first initiation as a farm pupil long ago. But I did lately repair a hedge, and very enjoyable it proved. Strictly speaking, the hedge was not a hedge, because nobody had touched it since 1937, so that the thing resembled a narrow forest, in places as high as a house. To start with, therefore, I marked each girth to a height of four feet above the ground; after two days of beating about the bush, sawing and hacking until a fringe appeared at the correct level, I was able to follow the example of John Clare's hedger who

> With sharp bill cuts the hazel bands,
> Then sits him down to warm his hands.

But the mass of dead wood did more than warm my hands; it comforted my stomach when I paused to cook dinner. Have *you* ever dined by starlight, in a frosty field, off sausages that were grilled over a flame? Have you ever tasted sweet cocoa that was boiled in a soup tin among red-hot ashes? If you have, your opinion of Claridges—though wholly admiring—will no longer be entirely envious. So there they lay, those circles of ash, those rings of fire, as though confirming Thomas Hardy's thoughts on Egdon Heath: "To light a fire is the instinctive and resistant act of man when, at the winter ingress, the curfew is sounded throughout Nature."

On the third day layering began; not according to the latest principles, but following my own. First, hazel stakes were inserted, about five feet high and a yard or so apart. These formed the lattice that would shape and bind the hedge. Next came the delicate task of so incising the timber that it would bend and interlace along the lattice. It all looks very simple; but if your switch-bill cuts too deep, the wood is either severed or left hanging by a ligament of bark; and if the blade cuts too shallow, the branch will not bend far enough. Co-ordination of eye and wrist must be instant, as with the athlete whom Robert Bridges admired:

> every perfect action hath the grace
> Of indolence or thoughtless hardihood.

It is almost true to say that the lower is the more important half of a hedge, and for two reasons; first, because it is the level at which gales attack the grass or other crop; second, because it is the level nearer to the ditches which must be kept clear in order to drain the field. Agriculture having become an industry, the whole business is bedevilled by the magic word 'efficiency', which we define according to the blindest demands of myopic greed. So many thousands of miles of hedgerows have been uprooted that Mammon is beginning to whine because its 'efficiency' has tilted the balance of Nature. Peering beyond next year's bank balance, one or two farmers are replanting their hedges. Unlike many insecticides, birds can kill pests without poisoning people. And although it is irrelevant to the Trade Gap, birds have a second advantage over insecticides; they sing.

Some people ask: "How many yards of hedge can be layered in a day?" But their question is unanswerable until you have discovered the condition of the hedge, the nature of its timber, the hours of work, and the weather itself. The hedge that occupied my own attention had to be felled before layering began, whereas the hedges on a well-kept estate may need only to be trimmed.

Although no mystery shrouds the craft of hedging, some shrubs and trees still create a mystique. For example, a servant who presented the first bunch of hawthorn on May Day received a bowl of cream from the farmer. In parts of Norfolk and Suffolk a few old people never will burn elder, because (they say) it was once used as a defence against witchcraft. But there is a more truly philosophical reason for not burning elder in the hearth; the stuff is likely to spit. Holly was for long regarded as a shield against misfortune. A sprig of ash—especially the rowan or mountain variety—was worn by carters who believed that it would protect their horses against black magic. Gilbert White mentions two Hampshire farmers who were required by ancient custom to provide oak for the yearly repair of village bowers. Some scholars set the beginnings of those traditions in the very earliest days of farming, when men cleared a patch in the forest. On that patch the holly and the whitethorn and the ash arose; and when the tree blossomed in spring, our forefathers accepted it as proof that the long nights and black frosts were over at last, and the miracle of seedtime and harvest once again assured.

Gentle and Simple

Despite the spirit of the age, class distinctions not only persist but
also proliferate their own variations. Even the housing estate has
an élite. I am not concerned to pronounce those social nuances as
good, or bad, or (like breathing) natural. I simply offer some
observations by one who finds himself in Scotland on Monday, in
Wales on Tuesday, and down in Devon on Wednesday. Thus,
although his novitiate may last longer than a doctor's, the veterinary surgeon lacks a GP's status in the village. Dentists, on the
other hand, fall midway between the two; and all are jockeying.
The doctor, for example, has lost ground because he is nowadays
a part-time unpensionable civil servant without paid holidays or
regulated hours of work. Worse still, he tends to combine with
several colleagues, to form a card-index relationship with thousands of so-much-per-head patients. The vet, by contrast, has
advanced. In the village of my childhood he entered the manor by
the servants' hall. Today he may be a JP and MFH.

Clergymen have everywhere slipped back, partly because they
are poorer than policemen, and partly because God has informed
the fashionable philosophers that He does not exist. However, one
aspect of theological precedence remains unchanged; a dissenting
minister is to the vicar as a vet to the doctor. Villagers ask: "Is he
a real parson?"—meaning, is he Church of England? The Roman
Catholic hierarchy remains an enigma to the uncommitted heirs of
Latimer and Ridley.

Despite their titles and surtax, stagefolk in deep country are
suspect. A younger son with one hunter and six hundred a year
impresses the older people in a way which Sir Garrick does not.
Brass is thinner than blood. Writers fare more fortunately, though
still with something of the condescension which first lionised
them during the eighteenth century. Poets, however, are classified
with elephants and other circus exhibits; the average countryman
being content with Sir Isaac Newton's definition of poetry as "an
ingenious sort of nonsense". Journalists have yet to make the
grade, both with the County and among cottagers, because rural
respectors of persons distrust publicity. To them the phrase
'private gentleman' seems tautological. For that reason editors

and anonymous contributors sometimes pass into respectability unnoticed.

Commissions in the armed forces retain much of their Georgian prestige. Service with the Territorial Army—favoured by eldest sons—tends to acquire the status of an honorary social degree. Here, strangely enough, the Senior Service gives way before the Army, no doubt because the latter is associated with families who led the mounted yeomanry regiments. A Commander in the hunting field looks somewhat at sea among so many Majors and half-Colonels. The Royal Air Force cuts little ice below the rank of Group-Captain. On the gilt-edged market, millionaires gain ground after initial take-over losses; Senators continue to expand; but dons are weak, and salesmen uncertain. Why do many stage-folk, financiers, prize-fighters, and politicians acquire a country estate? It cannot be solely as capital investment, for the absentee landlord incurs heavy overheads. Acres, it seems, are the best substitute for ancestry, as the Whig merchants knew when they bought-up Tory manors.

A Tudor countryman would have been utterly perplexed by our social snakes-and-ladders. He clung to rungs that had been approved by the mediaeval king who, in compiling a list of occupations, set the soldier at the top, and the lawyer and the businessman bracketed at the bottom. Older villagers share something of that perplexity whenever they meet certain members of the overpopulated City of Dreadful Knights: "I don't care whether yon's the Duke o' Timbuctoo. All I know is he used to sell gum-boots in't Bradford."

Scotland and Wales play their own variations on the social tune. A Cardiganshire hill-farmer may reveal complete disregard both of the snakes and of the ladders, as though to emphasise the history of a land of small and poor villages whose gentry long ago became Londonised, either by living there or by wishing they could. In the Scottish countryside there are still a few lairds who were not nurtured on the foreign fields of England; and the chief of a clan continues to exert something of a mystique not elsewhere to be found in Britain.

Shakespeare caused a man of King John's reign to deplore "the hurly-burly innovation" that was upsetting *l'ancien régime*. Happily for England, the "hurly-burly" never faltered, and is not faltering now. Anyone who knows the countryside closely, knows also that there has not been a social revolution in rural England, but only a lowering of standards, some of which were overdue to fall, while others have already brought us low in their decline. A financial revolution there has been, with cash pouring into the pockets of those who are most likely to squander it on trivial or harmful pursuits. Yet man's immemorial race to the social summit is not run solely in search of riches, for 'the best people' are faint echoes of Chaucer's "perfect gentle knight" who is not obsessed by the struggle for existence, and may therefore live graciously, according to the precept of Bishop Creighton: "Vulgarity is an inadequate conception of the art of living." We can admire the ideal of a gentleman; we can mock it, envy it, revile it; indeed, we can do almost anything except define it; though most of us recognise it when we meet it. Unlike the dodo, the ideal has survived by adapting to a changed environment. Writing of the year 1660, Macaulay observed: "When the lord of a Lincolnshire or a Shropshire manor appeared in Fleet Street he was as easily distinguished from the resident population as a Turk or a Lascar. His dress, his gait, his accent . . . marked him out as an excellent subject for the operations of swindlers . . . ." No modern lord of a manor is so conspicuous as that.

As Adam remarked to Eve: "We live in a time of change." Nevertheless, there seems no valid reason to suppose that Socialism has exterminated the farmhand whose son goes to a grammar school, whose grandson goes to a public school, and whose great-grandson, having bought an estate, lives the life which Tennyson saluted:

> And thus he bore without abuse
> The grand old name of gentleman,
> Defamed by every charlatan,
> And soiled by all ignoble use.

3

The Rough and the Smooth

"When two Englishmen meet," said Dr Johnson, "their first talk is of the weather." Such talk may appear absurd. After all, men and the weather have co-existed for some considerable time. The weather, however, outlives men, so that each generation is surprised by its fickle climate, and none ever wholly recovers from the shock; least of all the English, who in April may awake to a Shakespearean morning

> When icicles hang by the wall,
> And Dick the shepherd blows his nail,
> And Tom bears logs into the hall,
> And milk comes frozen home in pail. . . .

Our system of weather forecasting is relatively modern. Not until the end of the last century did farmers receive telegrams warning them of bad weather at haytime. But unofficial records have been kept for several centuries, and some of them make strange reading. Here is Gilbert White, writing in 1776: "two men had their fingers so affected by frost that mortification followed". And here is another parson, James Woodforde, writing from Norfolk in 1779: "It was like June today." Yet both those reports referred to a winter morning. Or consider this, by Dorothy Wordsworth: "It was very cold." And this, by Francis Kilvert: "Too hot to move." Each described a summer afternoon. But the point needs no emphasis. From Pepys to Richard Jefferies, our diarists ring the changes on the weather. And not only our diarists; from Julius Caesar to Alexandre Dumas, foreign observers have cursed our climate with an eloquence matching our own. Dean Swift equated what he regarded as a dearth of poets with what he imagined as a lack of sunlight:

> Say, Britain, could you ever boast
> Three poets in an age at most?
> Our chilling climate hardly bears
> A sprig of bay in fifty years.

One inclines to doubt that the English winter ever was so vile as it used to be. Science, certainly, can discover no drastic change in temperature. Yet some observers diagnose a very conspicuous difference. Seventy years ago E. V. Lucas cried: "Will the seasons ever readjust themselves or is the tendency of the future to push cold weather further and further into next year?" Nor is the topic solely one of conversation. It has crippled entire industries, and led some men to hang themselves. Thus, if you study the history of sheep-farming during the eighteenth century you will observe downward trends that were caused, not by incompetence, but by severe winters and wet summers. In 1702 a Somerset landowner, William Blathwayt of Dyrham Park, received a warning from his agent: "If it be a very frosty and snowey time the hay will be the dearer." On this same estate, a century later, one of the tenants could not pay his rent: "From the wetness of summer and the coldness and poorness of my land the loss of corn is very great." The truth is, any of the four seasons may at any time run untrue to form. Henley's July regatta has been obliterated by rain; Putney's April Boat Race has foundered in a blizzard; and now, as I write, the woods are brilliant with sunlight streaming through a clerestory of burnished boughs. The whole sky burns blue; not one white fleck on all its vast acreage. The garden wears a buttonhole culled from March and September; daisies, I see, and violas, and forget-me-nots, and one wallflower tilting the seedsman's calendar. Birds that lately haunted the dustbin now turn up their beak at a chicken sandwich, for frost and rain have rubbled the soil into a duff, teeming with the kind of plums which small birds relish. In the woods an hour ago the sun had polished the beeches to an olive green. Some of the fallen leaves shone like flames and then again like plump sparks flying upward as you rustled through them. On the opposite hill the whitewashed farm glistened as though it were an outsize mushroom; and you knew, from old acquaintance, that its Tudor beams glistened, too, dark as a whale's rump rinsed by many waters.

Like the wallflower, this mild weather confutes the text-books, and persuades a countryman to suppose that spring has arrived, bringing with it the music which Christina Rossetti overheard beside a copse

> Wherein on this whitethorn
> Singeth the thrush. . . .

Rivers give a new and gayer meaning to 'the blues'. Even the farmyard puddles catch the colour of the sky, mining those "little low heavens" that Gerard Manley Hopkins noticed on a bird's egg. Two days ago the heifers huddled against a bare hedgerow, seeking cold comfort from the wind. Now they loll in midfield while the warmth seeps through. Roused from their half-hibernation, squirrels scramble downstairs as though to answer Wordsworth's call:

> All things that love the sun are out of doors.

Yet up in Northumberland, or away in Sussex, the land may be swathed in mist or swaddled in snow. Landor took the rough with the smooth, and out of them made an Englishman:

> We are what Suns and Winds and Waters make us:
> The mountains are our sponsors and the rills
> Fashion. . . .

Sometimes these kindly days remain unclouded, even when their temperature sinks with the sun. Then you prolong your walk, and will forgo tea rather than miss one instant of a respite from rough weather, knowing that tomorrow, or next week, must put an end to such unseasonable smoothness. Meanwhile, sufficient unto the hour is the unexpectedness thereof; and having savoured it, you walk home with William Blake:

> The sun descending in the west,
> The evening star does shine;
> The birds are silent in their nest,
> And I must seek for mine.

A Mariner of England

The squall was visible, darkening the surface of the sea. Meeting it, the boat reared and plunged so steeply that her tinware clattered in the cabin. Having rounded the Point, I relaxed and glanced astern at the open sea, which had become a smudge of grey twilight and white waves. And there I saw a masthead that sank from sight and then again reared up and sank, crashing seaward into the night. It was the lifeboat, answering an equinoctial gale. Suddenly my own inshore buffeting seemed child's play.

Joseph Conrad, himself a master mariner, wrote an essay by way of an old man's war service, in which he described the work of the Dover Patrol. What he said then shall be my text now: "It's an odious thing to have to write in 'descriptive' fashion of men with whom one talked like a friend and found acceptance as one of themselves. If he sees these lines I hope he will forgive me."

My own 'he' was elderly yet so fresh that he gave life to a tired phrase—'Devon seadog'. But it would be wrong to locate him too closely, for he was a lifeboatman, one of a breed that plies all round Britain, from Land's End to John o' Groat's. At our first meeting I was impressed by his strength and his gentleness. I happen to be taller than most, yet whenever I talked with him I found myself looking up: not that he was a giant—six feet one or thereabouts—but the physical inch gained stature from its spiritual or intangible roots. As for his gentleness—which those huge fists belied—that was something you heard rather than saw, unless you found him in his garden, thinning the seedlings. Usually, however, the gentleness spoke for itself, slowly and in the deep notes that are music to all who love the West. He belonged to what Conrad called "the shy, silent type". But there was one subject which did test his restraint, and that was the people who wish to nationalise the lifeboatmen despite the fact that the men themselves prefer to remain as they are, rich because gain is not their landfall: "I've sailed the seas," my friend would say, "and our own boats are the best in the world. We don't want a rate-for-the-job. And we don't want no busybodies neither, hanging around and getting in the way."

He was sixty-five years old when I first met him; white-haired, blue-eyed, with pink cheeks so lightly touched by wind and worry that you would never suppose he had been twice ship-wrecked, and lost his only son at sea. In those years he was still a fisherman, still with the lifeboat, but already he had leased a smallholding against his retirement or 'beaching'. His wife came from Scotland, and of a line of Queens if her features told the truth. She pro-nounced 'snow' as 'snee', and always spoke of her husband as 'my man'.

Their cottage outshone the picture postcards. It was thatched, white-washed, festooned with roses, hollyhocks, honeysuckle. The path seemed permanently weedless; the borders shipshape; every grassblade in place. Indoors it was the same, though with-out any hint of the finicky. There was a barometer, of course, with oilskin and seaboots in a porch overlooking the cliff: no model ships, but a print of *The Wanderer* which Masefield had signed in 1930. Except during high summer, a fire burned in the hearth. When I asked him why, he smiled and said: "I sometimes think it comes o' having been wet so often."

The mariner had a good singing voice, and never tired of hear-ing his two favourite songs, "Home, Sweet Home" and "If You Were the Only Girl in the World". No man used foul language in his presence, but you could 'drat' the hammer that hit your thumb; and a pint of beer never harmed anybody. Having sunk one himself, he would sing about it:

> Ye mariners all, as you pass by,
> Call in and drink if you are dry.
> Call in and drink, nor think amiss,
> But pop your nose in a jug of this.

Concerning his own corner of the sea he was omniscient this side of infallibility. He knew where bass begged to be caught; where the low-tide fairway left three feet of water for small craft; where a misty headland forecast fine weather. In his sight, and therefore in his hands, a ship was indeed a She, a living creature, to be mastered, but never mishandled. Time has not yet outpaced his repertoire of knots, each with its apposite deftness. Forty years ago his cousin, a boat builder, made him an eight-foot mahogany praam for eight guineas, which included paddles and brass row-locks; the praam remains his grandson's pride.

In politics he voted Conservative because the Liberals were

D

doomed to come last in a field of three. In religion he was Anglican, but the wife being Calvinist, they had split the dogma by
joining the Wesleyans. "All the same," he confessed, "I do truly
love the proper Church. 'Tis th'only one with sailing orders, if
you understand." I understood that he loved the prayers for
those in peril and before a battle. On Christmas morning husband
and wife went ecumenically to the parish church, thereby acknow-
ledging the man's *patria potestas*.

His earthly god was King George V: "A seaman, sir. Would
have been admiral if the throne hadn't crossed his bows. I'd the
honour to be spoken by 'en. He must ha' liked the way I came
alongside 'cause he said, 'Coxswain, I see you know to luff.' So I
said, 'Aye, sir,' and then *he* said, 'Aye, sir.' And that was how I
spoke with King George." Of his more momentous conversations he never spoke at all unless you wearied him by trying to
extract the truth. And even then you got no dramatics. He might
have been describing a fly crawling up the window. Thus, when
he said, "There was a sea running," you knew that he referred to
the morning when he took the lifeboat into a Force 10 gale; and
when he said, "So we stood-by awhile," you knew that he referred
to the night when he kept watch over a listing tanker. He spent
most of the last war in minesweepers, having joined the Royal
Naval Reserve during the 1920s. On naval occasions the three
campaign medals shine alongside one for gallantry, another for
life-saving and a third for long service. Such are the men who, at
any hour of the day or night, stand ready and willing to defy
whatever wind may blow. The greater the need, the swifter the
response, for the brotherhood of the sea is an everlasting Yea.

Natives and Aliens

He seemed an amiable youth, doing what he called "a spot of
market research". The first question was: "How long have you
lived in this house?"

"Thirty-three years," I replied.

"Thirty-three?" He stared at me as though I were the Ancient
of Days. "You must be a sociological phenomenon."

It is true, of course, that more and more people are living fewer and fewer years in the same house. But it is also true that deep roots feed a countryman's conservatism, which is nowhere more conspicuous than in his attitude to strangers, and especially to strangers who have become his neighbours. Unlike a town, where no one knows the name of the people ten doors away, a village learns itself intimately, and tends to be less than effusive toward those whom it does not know intimately. Although that characteristic was very likely acquired in the years when the cave-next-door might turn nasty, it has been handed down through so many centuries that it must now be rated an inheritance. Nor is it indigenous to Britain; Émile Verhaeren noticed a similar trait in France: *"Les gens de bourgs vorsins sont dèja l'étranger. . . ."* Sometimes the aloofness seems no more than selfishness, as when Horace rebuked those of his fellow-Romans who refused hospitality to travellers in need. At all times and in all places there has been a reasonable dislike of the kind of newcomer who in our own time joins the parish council with a view to dominating it; the choir, because he wishes either to catholicise or to evangelise; and the Hunt, for whatever can be got from being seen with it. A subtler form of self-imposition occurs when the newcomer buys a playing field for the young villagers, and then accepts the chairmanship of the Playing Field Committee. A few newcomers remain permanently unaccepted because they have never offered themselves. They prefer to live in isolation, taking no part in any kind of parish business. When such hermits do relent, and join some of the hurly-burly, their native discretion may set them among the most trusted of the villagers.

A villager in deep country remembers that his grandfather left the place twice only—for the Boer War and for his operation, neither of which tempted him to repeat the process. Several elderly cottagers hereabouts have never seen the sea, though an old folks' outing would take them thither for a few shillings. Formerly the rule, such people are now, like myself, a sociological phenomenon.

For how long must a newcomer reside in the village before he is accepted as a villager? The answer to that question varies with the distance from a town. Within thirty miles of industrial areas the countryside has become so urban that strangers are no longer strange. Beyond that perimeter the urban influence dwindles. Even today there are villages where a stranger is sufficiently novel to seem worth staring at. Many old villagers are slow to accept a newcomer. Some are so slow that they impose a novitiate of twenty years. A few never do accept anyone who is not a native. To them even the man from five miles away seems an alien. That was the attitude of Victorian Cornishfolk who described as 'foreign' all visitors from beyond the Tamar. And the attitude is still alive. A friend of mine, having lived in a Cornish hamlet for six years, was told by his charwoman that she preferred to work for "local people". Hill-dwellers are notoriously clannish. Venerable farmers in my part of the world regard the valley as "the folks living down there".

The summit of seclusion is reached in Welsh-speaking Wales and the Gaelic Highlands. There no stranger ever does take root. He remains separated from the natives by a chasm of centuries. His children may advance halfway across that chasm, and his grandchildren may set foot upon the far side of it, but he himself must live and die beyond the pale. Nor is his destiny confined to townsmen, for villagers, too, can quarrel with their environment. Hillfolk settling in a vale find the scene dull; valefolk moving to a hill find the height intimidating. Sailors crave the sea, and will, if they can, retire within sight of it, even though the glimpse be no more than the mirage of telescopic imaginings which Eustacia Vye's brass-buttoned father indulged when he walked on Egdon Heath.

Some creatures became extinct because their ability to adapt was deficient; others—like the giraffe—adapted in ways that were too highly-specialised for a more general evolution. It is not for our generation to know whether man will achieve a compromise between his old need of roots and his new urge for horizons. That no such compromise has yet been achieved is evident to any doctor, any policeman, and indeed to everyone who is not grinding a boomerang and then trying to pass it off as a dove. Meanwhile the chronicler of country life must report a national dichotomy; on the one hand, millions of people uprooting themselves every decade; on the other, a few hardy perennials who at a ripe age die in the village that was their birthplace and an abiding home.

How might those veterans define the gulf between a newcomer and themselves? Somewhat as follows: no man is truly a member of our village unless he can sift the blackbird's song from a thrush's imitation of it; unless he can recognise a medlar, a coulter, and kale; unless he knows that the late doctor's sister-in-law drank gin from a bottle marked *As Prescribed*; unless he worships in church now and again, and sometimes attends a meet of the foxhounds; unless he remembers when the brook ran dry, when the bridge was flooded, when the Royal car passed by, and when Ernie's two-year-old won the Cup from the favourite. A stranger (the veterans might add) will remain a stranger until he has learned that Astronaut Terrace was formerly Spotted Cow Lane; that it is now eleven years since a disputed right-of-way caused the Admiral to consign the curate to Coventry; that the earliest bluebells are to be found in Timothy's Copse; and that Timothy was old Fred's cousin, who hanged himself in young Bert's barn. All that may sound a tall order, yet I can produce a taller, for there are countryfolk who would insist that no man is truly a villager unless, as a child, he saw the sun rise above the church, and, as a grandfather, watched it set below the smithy.

Down the Primrose Path

Once upon a time I discovered Primroseland. You will not find that name on the map because the christening took place privately and unrecorded. I had been walking the heathy plateau from Nether Stowey to Crowcombe at the foot of the Quantocks; and having crossed a railway, I followed the lane towards Wiveliscombe, through a wood. Now all woodland lanes are full of wonder, but that lane was pressed down and overflowing, for it wore a ribbon of grass along the middle, and the ribbon shone with primroses. But that was not all. Presently the flowers spilled from the lane into the wood itself, spreading a yellow carpet farther than the eye could see.

My own Primroseland was only one of many that have been discovered by wayfarers. Perhaps the most eminent springtime explorer was John Donne, who, while visiting the Herberts at Montgomery, was so entranced by the primroses on Castle Hill that he composed a poem which baptised the place:

> Upon this Primrose hill,
> Where, if Heav'n would distil

A shower of rain, each several drop might go
To his own primrose, and grow Mana so. . . .

After three centuries the flowers still abound on that hill.

Some people prefer primroses when they grace the banks of
lanes. Certainly it is delightful to walk accompanied by posies.
Yet to my own mind the flower looks best in a wood, where its
beauty is both humbled and heightened by the fan-vaulted roof
and slender pillars. And of all woods a beech is best; translucent
in spring, flamboyant in autumn. And of all beechwoods the best
are to be found in the Chiltern Hills of Buckinghamshire and
Oxfordshire.

Unlike a bird's eye primrose, which thrives among our northern
mountains, the common variety *vulgaris* craves a mild winter. That
is why the South-west bears the largest and most prolific flowers.
I once transplanted a primrose from Cornwall to the Chilterns,
curious to discover how it would respond. The plant bloomed,
but was only two-thirds of its former size. Next year I took the
migrant down to Heddon's Mouth in Devonshire, and there it
grew large again.

I used to make regular journeys across Alston Fell, that mighty
realm where Cumberland greets Northumberland. As the car
climbs each hairpin bend, so the trees grow sparser and more
stunted; but at about a thousand feet—where the trees give up—
there you will find primroses. They flower as a rule in late April,
six weeks after the March unfolding in South Devon. During
May I have seen them bent by a blizzard, as though to verify
Dorothy Wordsworth's *Journal* for 15th May 1802: "It snowed
this morning just like Christmas."

England has several sorts of primrose. John Parkinson cited
four in his gardening book of 1629. A thrum-eyed primrose
(thrum meaning 'thread') has its stamen above the stigma; in a
pin-eyed primrose the stamen is below the stigma. The petals
are borne on stalks which appear to rise separately, from the root,
but if you look closely you will notice a common stalk among the
leaves.

A jealous rival said of Nicholas Culpeper that "he understood
not the Plants he trod upon". But even the Latinless man recog-
nises a primrose as *prima rosa*, the first flower of spring ('rose'
being an old name for any kind of flower). "O rare primrose,"

cried W. H. Davies, "born when the spring winds blow." Yet a
primrose is also the last flower of spring, flourishing in the cold
north-east until the brink of summer, and among some gardens at
Michaelmas or on New Year's Day. Shakespeare perceived the
dangers that dwell in dalliance. Twice he uttered a warning to
wantons. Ophelia, you remember, shuns "the primrose paths of
dalliance"; and in *Macbeth* the portentous porter wags an even
more admonishing tongue: "The primrose way to th'everlasting
bonfire." Though I write without his book, I fancy Gilbert White
does not mention primroses. Richard Jefferies, on the other hand,
lived for their light, and knew where to find it: "in Sussex, round
about the Hurst of the Pierrepoints, primroses are to be seen
soon after the year has turned." Writing in February, Keats
could only imagine what Jefferies had discovered in January:
"The simple flowers of spring are what I want to see again."

You would scarcely believe that genial men could quarrel about
flowers, yet they do. I have watched a Cornishman grow red in the
face when a Devonian claimed that the finest primroses are to be
seen at a bend in the road between Barnstaple and Blackmoor
Gate. And both men would have refuted the shepherd who
assured me that the flower does best above Dunster in Somerset.
At least their debate avoids the myopia of "Peter Bell":

> A primrose by a river's brim
> A yellow primrose was to him,
> And it was nothing more.

Benjamin Disraeli ("We authors, Ma'am") caused one of his
characters to say: "Primroses make a capital salad." To which an
indignant lady replied: "Barbarian!" Primroses, in fact, were
Disraeli's favourite flower; and when he died his admirers founded
the Primrose League to ensure "the maintenance of religion, of
the estates of the realm, and of the imperial ascendancy of Great
Britain". The league's badge had the letters PL surrounded by
primroses. In 1884 there were 957 members; thirty years later
there were nearly three million. Beatrix Potter recalled a flowery
occasion in 1884:

> On Primrose Day [she wrote] four gentlemen drove up in a four-
> wheeler to the Beaconsfield Statue. They wished to place a large
> wreath round its shoulders, but a policeman rather spoiled the cere-
> mony by bundling them off to the Station on the charge of desecrat-

ing public buildings. Having been detained during two hours they returned to the Statue, and with the help of a fishing-rod triumphantly hoisted the wreath to its place.

But the primrose transcends politics, for it dwells among that greater company which led Robert Bridges to wonder and to worship:

> Thou tender flower,
> I kneel beside thee,
> Wondering why God
> So beautified thee.

Death of a Village

By any standard the village was beautiful. Its narrow street contained well-preserved Tudor houses and one or two from the Middle Ages. London lay nearly forty miles away, and a journey into the City took the better part of two hours. A handful of people did commute, but the rest worked at or near their home, and many were farmfolk.

During the 1950s, however, the village began to show disturbing symptoms. Commercial travellers took to using the street as a short cut, which meant that the street became a main road. More commuters arrived, bristling the station with briefcases. Meadows fetched many pieces of silver, not because the natives needed houses, but because the strangers demanded dormitories. Yet still the village remained a beautiful place, set among hills, watered by a stream. Unfortunately, they destroyed the stream in order to provide water for immigrants, leaving the villagers to share Oliver Goldsmith's sorrow:

> No more thy glassy brook reflects the day,
> But choked with sedges, works its weedy way.

Then even the "weedy way" ran dry, and only a green hollow showed where the fishes had fed.

Unfortunately, too, the commercial travellers so multiplied that a by-pass had to be built because the village could no longer cope with the cars. This by-pass might have been a blessing, but proved only a disguise, for it was linked to the village by a shorter by-pass which lay like a scar on the heart. The larger by-pass separated the church from the village, so a poker-face bridge was built across the traffic, leaving the church deafened and divided. From 8.30 a.m. until 7 p.m. the High Street was a permanent car park. Elderly pedestrians dithered on the kerb, seeking a lull amid the roar which drowned their conversation.

Villagers hoped for some respite when the place was declared part of an area of outstanding natural beauty, protected by an Act of Parliament which encouraged the preservation of hale old houses. The effect of that Act was interesting: somebody promptly

pulled down a hale old house, and built a block of flats on the site—country life with a window-box, but no garden. The old countryfolk died, and were not succeeded by sufficient young ones. Again Oliver Goldsmith set the scene:

> Ill fares the land, to hast'ning ills a prey,
> Where wealth accumulates, and men decay. . . .

During the 1960s the slow steam trains were replaced by fast diesels, so that the tide of Londoners became a flood. Next, the motor trade drove up, competing with itself across a few yards of road (today the parish has half-a-dozen garages). Soon after that, somebody demolished a seventeenth-century house—the finest of its kind in the High Street—and converted the space into a bank. So now the village has three banks. One assumes there are enough overdrafts to go round.

In due course another handsome old house was destroyed—this time causing an outcry in the Press. For two years the site was a Golgotha of weeds, gravel, bricks, plaster. There also a block of flats arose to clash with the hills above them. Today a platoon of estate agents advertise 'Executive Homes' and all the vulgar Jonesmanship which that meaningless phrase incites. Charles Lamb made a fair comment when he deplored the "brick-and-mortar process of destruction". The process itself is at least as old as the Industrial Revolution, that curious form of house-keeping whereby we agreed to become unable to feed ourselves. John Ruskin described the Victorian phase of the process: "Wherever I travel in England," he wrote, "I see that men have no desire or hope, but to have large houses and to be able to move fast. Every perfect and lovely spot which they can touch they defile." But Mammon—which disregards any voice except its own—lately received a warning from an American family who used to visit the village during their holidays: "We shan't come any more," they told a newspaper reporter. "The place has been ruined."

A twisting lane leads from the village, parts of it so narrow that two lorries must proceed warily. I used to walk there, and was amazed if I met four vehicles an hour. Now the lane is so dangerous that many people refuse to walk along it; some decline even to drive. In order to keep up with the times the council inserted a stretch of wide road—known locally as 'the mini-mile'—where speeds of seventy are common among maniacs racing for first place at the narrow bend.

Does one weep, or should one laugh, at the concrete name-plates that have been tacked onto lanes through woods? What *is* the appropriate response when a comely brick-and-flint building is demolished in order to make way for the angular bungalows which now deface what used to be part of the abbey? To say "But people must live somewhere" does not answer the question. It begs it.

Once famed for its dahlias, the railway station has become a
rush-hour queue of crowding-room-only, and the empty flower
beds yield a crop of fag-ends. Many of the country people have
fled, some of them at a time of life when it is painful and perhaps
impossible to take root in a strange soil. Even the badgers have
gone, seeking new pastures and old quietude. The rest of the
inhabitants occupy a nether-world, not quite in nor ever wholly
out of London. In short, the village has become a suburb. Now
suburbs are sometimes inevitable and occasionally pleasant. Like
the people who dwell there, they play a leading role in modern
life. But to a village they bring death; and anyone who pretends
otherwise is equating 'life' with shops, season tickets, and estate
agents. Of course, the village is only one among thousands that
now lie within reach of an industrial octopus. All are a sign of the
times, and none of them needs to ask for whom the bell tolls.
The issue is not whether, but in what manner, the old order shall
change and give way to a new.

It would be interesting to debate whether the degeneration of
the countryside ought to be checked and confined; even more
interesting to debate whether it *can* be checked and confined.
But that is not what I set out to do. My task was to announce the
death of Great Missenden in Buckinghamshire.

Shank's Pony

"I nauseate walking. 'Tis a country diversion." So said the lady in
Congreve's *Way of the World*. And her way has become our way,
though not Ben Jonson's, who walked from London to Scotland
in order to reduce his weight (which he estimated as "twenty
stones less two pounds"). Britons, in short, have returned to the
slothful snobbery which dismayed a German visitor, Pastor
Carl Philip Moritz, when he made a walking tour through
England two centuries ago: "A traveller on foot in this country,"
he complained, "seems to be considered as a sort of wild man
who is to be stared at, pitied, suspected, and shunned."

Walking for pleasure resembles the age of steam; it was born
toward the end of the eighteenth century, and died in the mid-
twentieth. Yet what memorable athletes stalked that brief era.

De Quincey reckoned that Wordsworth, when he was sixty-five, had walked 180,000 miles. John Buchan once walked sixty-one miles in twenty-four hours. Hilaire Belloc created an unbroken record by walking from Carfax to Marble Arch in something over eleven hours. All those men walked for pleasure. Among the walkers for profit was William Gale, who in 1877 covered 1,500 miles in a thousand consecutive hours, halting only when he fell asleep.

Which are the best walking seasons? The less hardy wayfarer tends to emerge at Easter; but a true walker, an all-the-year-rounder, accepts Meredith's advice: "We should love all changes of weather." Meredith might have added: "And each of the twenty-four hours." To set out from Veryan by lamplight, and to reach Fowey by sunlight, is to understand what Traherne meant when he said: "Eternity was Manifest in the Light of the Day, and som thing infinit Behind evry thing appeared. . . ."

Where are Britain's best walking regions? Having tramped in every county of England and Wales, and in most of Scotland's, I divide the going into the rough and the smooth. The latter is to be found wherever a lane creates it; the former belong rather to moorlands and mountains, some of which have been partly tamed. I think of the Pennine Way, our longest footpath, following the roof of northern England for 250 miles, from Edale in Derbyshire to Kirk Yetholm in Roxburghshire. Most of the Way is a thousand feet above the sea; some of it is two thousand feet above; once, it exceeds three thousand. A gentler journey follows the Thames, which I tracked from Teddington to its source in a meadow near Cirencester. Acre for acre, however, it is Buckinghamshire that contains more footpaths than any other British county; and every one of them is signposted. Nowhere else in the kingdom will you find the intimate spaciousness, the unfailing surprise around the next bend, which proclaim the Chiltern Hills of Buckinghamshire and Oxfordshire. But, of course, every county deserves to be walked. I remember the hills of Galloway, where I marched all day, feeling that I was the man before Adam. I remember the grassy Peddars Way and the Norfolk gipsies pitching a lonely caravan there. I remember those quietest lanes under the sun, westward from Severn to Clun Forest . . . the green roads of Honington and Idlicote, which Shakespeare may have followed . . . the path from Heddon's

Mouth to Woody Bay, with the sea on one side, and Exmoor on the other . . . the day-long trek from Helmsdale to John o'Groat's via Forsinard, along a lane too narrow for cars to pass one another . . . Sarn Helen, the Roman way through Welsh mountains . . . the beech-clad switchback from Cobblers Hill to Hotley Rise near John Hampden's old home in the Chilterns . . . the avenue of sea-sprayed trees from Gerrans to St Anthony Lighthouse in Cornwall . . . Dartmoor's trackless solitude beyond Peter Tavey . . . and the No Through lane to Bulpot Farm above Kirkby Lonsdale in Westmorland.

A motorist watches the car ahead, and cannot safely look where he is going. The windscreen reveals Britain in little bits. But walking exceeds the sum of its parts, for it enters churches and castles and inns; it leans over bridges; it rests beside brooks; and, by parsing the place-music of country talk, it overhears—as Quiller-Couch overheard—the heart of rural England

> like a psalm
> Of green days telling with a quiet beat.

Some men walk alone while their thoughts, like Masefield's, lie fallow until the moment that shall arrive

> To consecrate the spirit and the hour,
> To light to sudden rapture, and console. . . .

Others travel companionably, like Chaucer's pilgrims:

> Wel nyne and twenty in a companye,
> Of sondry folk, by aventure y-falle
> In felawshipe, and pilgrims were they alle . . .

One or two prefer to work while they wander, like Hobbes, who (according to his friend, John Aubrey) anticipated Captain Cuttle's advice: "He walked much and contemplated, and he had in the head of his cane a pen and ink-horn, and carried always a note-booke in his pocket, and as soon as a thought darted, he presently entered it in his booke, or otherwise might have lost it." And of course there are those privy counsellors who, having walked hand-in-hand, take their ease with J. M. Synge:

> In a nook
> That opened south,
> You and I
> Lay mouth to mouth.

Charles Lamb, the unmarried man, might have described all such explorers as "walkers who are not walkers".

The elect among pilgrims are the thirty-miles-a-day-men who follow a physiological pathway to Paradise. How often has a long march brought me, as it brought Edward Thomas,

> to the borders of sleep,
> The unfathomable deep
> Forest where all must lose
> Their way . . . .

Each, then, to his taste, for G. M. Trevelyan spoke from experience when he said of walking: "It is a land of many paths and of no-paths, where every one goes his own way and is right."

4

Songs before Sunrise

It was still dark and rather cold, so I stopped by the roadside, and entered a field where I made a fire of sticks, on which I heated some coffee. No moon shone, and the stars seemed to swim, hiding and seeking among clouds.

Precisely where I was I did not know, but Time had ceased to matter, so my wrist-watch ticked unnoticed while the fire glowed like an hospitable sun, deepening the darkness. Presently I put out the blaze, and with the last brand lit a pipe. Having done so, I returned to the car, through that faint lessening of gloom which precedes the dawn. And then something happened. You might call it something remarkable, were it not that the event occurs every day throughout the year; a lark began to sing; tremulous as first, but gaining confidence as it soared. John Davidson caught the moment:

> Low, low it whispers; stays and goes;
> It comes again; again takes flight;
> And like a subtle presence grows
> And almost gathers into sight.

I stood still, swivelling my head like a blind man in search of the sound. But you cannot scan a poem while it dims a star; so in the end I lowered my gaze, and was content to hear the unseen. Surely a dawning skylark excels the moonlit nightingale? Young Keats heard the nightingale, and was sad:

> My heart aches, and a drowsy numbness pains
> My sense. . . .

E

But Meredith in his age pronounced a different verdict on the lark: "He is joy."

Now my nose was dripping, and I remembered those other aspects of reality which are commonly mistaken for the whole . . . petrol from a garage, razor blades from the chemist. I ushered the dog into the car, and was about to switch-on the ignition when I found myself blinking. One sometimes does, without at first understanding why. My hand was already on the key. Had I turned it, I must have missed an experience which not even the calendar could promise to repeat. As it was, I withdrew my hand, and waited. After a while I looked up again, and this time I saw that an enormous building had arisen. It was Stonehenge.

Minute by minute, as though awakened by that skylark, the silhouette grew clearer until at length each plinth stood out against the stars, like a prophetic fingerpost to Heaven. I felt as though I were at a theatre wherein the curtain had risen on an empty stage, and in the background a dark sky turned pale while the invisible electrician performed a miracle. How many times in his life, I wondered, was a traveller likely to pitch his caravan without forethought in darkness, and at dawn to find himself under the shadow of prehistory's classic monument? Stevenson had experienced a similar gratitude when he watched sunrise from the Lozère: "I felt I was in someone's debt for all this liberal entertainment. And so it pleased me, in a half-laughing way, to leave pieces of money on the turf as I went along, until I had left enough for my night's lodging."

Prices are not what they used to be, and I therefore refrained from casting my own daily bread upon the waters of oblivion; but I did forget about the dripping nose, the petrol, the stubble. I thought only of the skylark's remote ancestor who had sung the self-same song, not above a ruined temple, but to a city of stone which fur-clad men had ferried and hauled from the Prescelly Hills in south-west Wales. Siegfried Sassoon asked and answered the question:

> What is Stonehenge? It is the roofless past;
> Man's ruinous myth; his uninterred adoring
> Of the unknown. . . .

In 1915 the "roofless past" was sold for £6,600 to Sir Cecil Chubb, who in 1918 gave it to the nation; by 1970 the National Trust had acquired nearly 1500 acres of adjacent farmland. Scholars still wrangle over the purpose of Stonehenge, but science has dispelled some myths. The Heel Stone, for example, does not mark the point of sunrise on Midsummer Day; that cannot happen until the year 3260. When Stonehenge was built the point of sunrise lay further to the west. It seems certain, however, that the stones were raised to salute the gods.

The gods themselves smiled on that April dawn, for soon the rest of the birds responded, even as those Celts had responded

when, with their soul for sextant, they too aspired toward the light. One by one the thrush and the blackbird, the robin and wren, sang their songs before sunrise while the plain lay so still that every distant copse and hedge sent its own audible choir.

Science does well to warn us that we must not project human emotion onto birds. More conspicuously even than men, the animal creation is a slave of Necessity. Nevertheless, we translate the dawn chorus literally, into our own language of joy, and are uplifted by it. Do any other creatures start their day with such jubilation? Do any others work so hard? Imagination can scarcely conceive the bird-hours that are spent ferrying food to those fledgling beaks; neither can it count the acts of self-sacrifice that are made in the name of 'instinct'. Truly we have acquired an impressive knowledge of our ignorance.

Meanwhile I returned to the circle of charred sticks, for this was neither the time nor the place to be sitting at the wheel of a car. Slowly the eastern sky was lit by the lamps of day, Homer's "rosy-fingered dawn". Where I had lately crouched in darkness, there now I lay in light while the cuckoo told a new time of year.

The song of the cuckoo is both *Ave* and *Salve*, for it greets a new season and bids adieu to the golden host of times past. And if we are wise as well as fortunate, the moments which lie all around will seem so sweet that they soften the parting from those other moments which lie far behind. So, as I lay on Salisbury Plain, listening to the cuckoo, I learned with Wordsworth that youth's *temps perdu* is not beyond recall:

> And I can listen to thee yet,
> Can lie upon the Plain
> And listen, while I do beget
> That golden time again.

Tea in the Backwoods

I suddenly remembered his invitation. "Come back one day," he had said, "and we'll have another chat." ('Chart' he pronounced it, being a Chiltern man and therefore one of the few who really do say 'oi' in place of 'I'). So back I went, along an overgrown path into the woods, and found his cottage, so tumbled-down that on first sighting it, three months ago, I had blinked when an occupant appeared—an elderly eremite bachelor.

He recognised me at once, and seemed pleased, as well he might, because not many southern homes are so secluded.

"You've come at the roight toime," he said. "Oi was just going to make a cup."

So I sat down, on a collapsible chair beneath peeling wallpaper, and remarked that his tenancy of sixty years must have witnessed much change.

"Change?" He glanced up, rather as though change might be

hanging from the rafters. "Oi aren't seen no change. Not round these parts. Anyway, if your'e hinterested in 'istory, you'll know already, this is one o' the very oldest districts in England."

"Really?"

"Ah, the vicar's told me about it. Says it was conquered by a fella called Norman." He paused, as though something were not quite right. "Anyow, the fella wrote a book about it. The book of domesday. Oi've not read it meself. Oi can't git down the library loike wart oi used. Did you ever meet 'im?"

"Norman?"

"The vicar."

"I did, actually. About a year ago."

"Real good sort, the vicar. Do you know wart 'ee said to me once? 'Ee said, the trouble with the Church of England is you can't never laugh in it 'cause if you do someone'll tap you on the shoulder and say, 'Remember where you are'." Again he paused. "Funny, thart. You can weep as much as you loike—more the better if it's a funeral—but if you laugh when they bring glad tidings of great joy. . . . Fancy you knowing the vicar. Did 'ee ever tell you 'is tale?"

"Which one was that?"

"About when 'ee were vicar of . . . oi can't remember the name . . . the church 'ad six bells. Ding-dong, ding-dong, ding-dong. Just loike thart. And every one different. Anyow, the vicar were passing the church one day while the bells was ringing, and 'ee noticed a visitor, just nodding and enjoying 'isself. So the vicar goes up to 'im and says, 'Aren't our bells beautiful?' And the visitor says, 'Wart?' So the vicar says it again, 'Aren't our bells beautiful?' And the visitor shakes 'is 'ead and says, 'Speak up. Oi can't 'ear you above them blasted bells'." Once again he paused. "When the vicar told me thart, oi near fell orf me chair."

"Did he tell you any others?"

"Plenty. But thart was the only religious one. You interested in religion?"

"I think we all ought to be."

"Oi've booked me own place. Way up agin the church gate. Oi goes and sits there sometoimes, just 'aving a think." He leaned toward me. "Wart do *you* think?"

"Many brave men have believed," I said, "and many wise ones, too."

"Thart's the way oi look at it. 'Taint a problem you can solve out o' books. Oi always remember something my old mother used to say . . . ' 'ope, 'eave and 'elp. And the greatest of these,' she said, 'is charity'." He glanced at the hearth. "Is thart old kettle leaking again? But talking o' religion, oi once knowed a charp as worked for a barber when 'ee were a kid, sixpence a week lathering. And this 'ere barber 'ee warn't much good 'cause 'ee knowed that if the fellas didn't loike 'im they'd to pushboike ten moile to one as they did. Anyow, a regular customer come in one day, saying 'eed been to Rome, and got in with some pilgrims, and they all kneeled while the Pope blessed 'em. 'Ah,' 'ee said, 'and wart's more,' 'ee said, 'the Pope spoke to everyone of us. And do you know wart he said to me while oi were kneeling' 'Well?' says the barber. 'Well,' says the customer, 'the Pope looked down at me and 'ee said, Gawd, what a 'orrible 'aircut'."

Then we discussed wages.

"When my grandard were a nipper 'ee used to walk six moile to work. And in them years it *was* work, twelve-hour-a-day, starting at six. So thart meant 'eed to leave 'ome soon arter four. And then 'eed to walk bark again. Oi don't suppose 'ee sat down to 'is supper afore eight. And wart did 'ee git for it? Six bob a week."

"The cost of living. . . ."

"Living always was expensive for them as can't afford it."

"Agreed," I nodded. "Even so, some of the modern youngsters. . . ."

"You don't need to tell me about thart. Oi'd a real load of junk up 'ere only last week. Think they must ha' lorst the way to London. Loike a pack o' hapes they was, grinning through their curls, and every hape with one o' them musical boxes they all carry. Talk about noise! Ah, and oi don't loike it no more'n you do. But afore oi starts preaching too loud, oi always thinks o' my old grandard . . . twelve-moile-a-day, twelve-hour-a-day, twelve-pence-a-day. Ah, and 'ee couldn't put thart in 'is poipe and smoke it 'cause 'ee 'adn't got 'is penny for the shag."

Again I nodded.

"Oi aren't Labour, mind. Pack o' troublemakers, thart's all they are nowadays. And oi aren't Liberal party neither 'cause oi don't reckon it is a party. Still, there's toimes oi think the Good Book was roight. A camel's got to open its eyes very woide indeed if a rich man warnts to git through.'

"It is strange," I murmured.

"Everything's strange. Whenever oi walk down the lane, and see a little bird lying dead in the snow, oi feel real sorry. It don't seem to make sense. All thart trouble, breeding them feathers and the song, and then one wintry day . . . 'old on, though . . . thart vicar we was talking about . . . oi've just remembered another of 'is religious ones. . . ."

A Charm of Harbours

How pleasant it is to savour the many-mingled cargoes that pass through a small harbour—the rope, resin, corn, tar, apples, petrol, pigs. Despite a modern costume, the scene remains much the same as when George Crabbe watched a vessel unloading at Aldeburgh:

> The lumbering wealth she empties round the place,
> Package and parcel, hogshead, chest, and case:
> While the loud seaman and the angry hind,
> Mingling in business, bellow to the wind.

When next you do visit such a place, seek out its customs house or harbour office, for it will be among the most impressive buildings in town. At Poole it is an eighteenth-century house, formerly a club, where sea captains sipped sherry while doing business with the local merchants. From its windows you survey a bustle of small ships, cobbled quays, weathered stanchions, wheeling gulls.

If you define a harbour as any place having a jetty for sea-going vessels, then Britain's smallest harbour must surely be at Boscastle on the north coast of Cornwall. Though I was there many times, I never measured the width of its fairway. In calm weather a lifeboat might squeeze herself through, but when the wind is off the sea, only a torpedo could put out. Cornwall, indeed, is a kingdom of little harbours. Their names sing a shanty: Polperro, St Mawes, Fowey, Padstow, Portscatho, Mousehole, Mevagissey. Throughout the year their boats bobble, the gulls call, lobsters or China clay await despatch, and at low water you notice a castaway, downward bound for Lyonesse. My father once told me that in his Cornish childhood the Breton fishermen sailed across to St Mawes at regatta time. There was, he said, a

lingua franca or ancient Celtic sea-patois which enabled the two
races to make some sense of each other. In the Orkneys, which
were Scandinavian territory until the Middle Ages, Swedish and
Norwegian currency is still accepted as legal tender by shopkeepers serving the fishing fleets.

Britain is girdled with small harbours. They box the compass
from Wick to Winchelsea, from Fishguard to Bridport, from
Whitehaven to Dale. Some of them are regionally unique—
Arnside, for instance, which is Westmorland's only seaside place—

and many are inshore harbours, good pull-ups for coastmen.
Others send their ships across the world. At Fowey I have heard a
German bo'sun arguing in English with a Spanish radio operator.
At Glasson (the old port of Lancaster) I have played draughts with
a Swede who could not, and with a Welshman who would not,
speak English.

Some people remember the years when our coasting vessels
were as much a part of the rural scene as the blacksmith and
carpenter who built them. Like the Cornish harbours, the names

of those vanished vessels sing a song of the sea: Brixham trawler, Hastings lugger, Bristol cutter, Norfolk wherry, Mersey flat, Thames bawley, Falmouth punt, Morecambe nobby, Langstone ketch, Brighton hoggy, Orkney skiff, Rye smack, Yorkshire coble, Plymouth hooker. Many of the vessels were owned and sailed by local families who fetched and carried between harbours where now only a gull comes: Lydney, Gatcombe, Porlock, Quay, Old Carlisle. When that tradition foundered, it took with it the breed of coastwise seamen whom Andrew Marvell admired:

> Thus sang they, in the English boat,
> An holy and a cheerful note;
> And all the way, to guide their chime,
> With falling oars they kept their time.

Small harbours have built famous ships, like the *Result* of Barnstaple, a three-masted top-sail schooner, launched in 1893, which was bought by a group of seamen at Braunton, a village on the River Taw (in 1850 the village contained half-a-dozen master-mariners). Having plied between Antwerp and the west country, the *Result* became HMS *Q23*, an armed sailing ship of the 1914 War. Commanded by Lieutenant (afterwards Rear-Admiral) P. J. Mack, she engaged an enemy submarine off the Dogger Bank, with gunfire so accurate that it killed the German captain and three of his ratings.

Some harbours have silted up, as at Tregoney in Cornwall, which used to serve Falmouth and the English Channel, but is now an inland village. Two centuries ago Daniel Defoe remarked on Tregoney's decline: "A town", he wrote, "of very little trade." Dunster is another seaport that became high and dry. Now only a signpost to Dunster Beach recalls the medieval quay from which the lord of the manor, Sir Hugh Luttrell, sailed in the *Leonard of Dunster*, accompanied by five oxen and two pipes of ale. Another Exmoor harbour—Porlock Weir—became a commercial disaster. The venture had been planned by a Victorian industrialist who hoped to transform Exmoor into a wasteland of lead and copper mines; *sed Deus flavit*. The desecration petered out, and Porlock Weir escaped the prosperous plight of Barry.

From time to time I visit John o' Groat's in Caithness, which is as far north as you can go without getting your feet wet. Always I pause a little to the south, at Helmsdale, formerly a thriving fishing harbour. When I last went there, one old man was painting one old dinghy while one old trawler dozed in the sun. Watchet, by contrast, is about to boom because, during the 1970s, several million sterling will be spent on enlarging the quay; yet it is not many years since the arrival of a three-hundred-ton coaster was rated good business.

Many of our small harbours stand in beautiful countryside. What is lovelier than Lynmouth and the green heights above it, bulwarks of Exmoor and the Severn Sea, gateway to the Atlantic. There indeed the words of Charles Kingsley come true: "What a sea-wall they are, those Exmoor hills! Sheer upward from the sea a thousand feet. . . ." Poised between two worlds, such places are naturally amphibious. Gum-boots answer to the name of sea-boots; the floor is the deck; and among local weathermen the Meteorological Office cuts less ice than it forecasts. Sailors discuss corn with farmers who grow it on the cliffs above the jetty; farmers discuss fairways with sailors who seek them through the shoals below the lighthouse. And at the quayside inn after dark, while ships tug at their chain, and water sidles past, a youth who has sailed around the world learns about the footpaths from an old man who has never left his county.

The Colour of Life

Easter falls at a moment when the curtain is rising on a new scene. The year itself, of course, contains several changes of scene; leaves turn brown and fall away; snow spreads a silent mantle. But all those changes are either transient or gradual. They span no single week during which the look of the land is transformed. In April, however, one week does transform the land; and green is the dominant colour.

Deciduous plants follow the tempo of their aspect and altitude. I have seen the Severn at Llanidloes when every hedgerow was in leaf; and having climbed toward Plynlimon, I found all buds as tight as the proverbial fist. Within a few yards of the Thames near Eynsham there is a hill whose trees are bare for at least a week after the riverside leaves have opened. On high ground in northern counties you may pass what appears to be fallow tilth, but if you glance back at it, with the sun in your eyes, you will detect the oats, speckled like mustard-and-cress on brown bread. Down in Devon no second glance is needed, for the wheat glows greener than the grass and taller.

Spring's regional timetables are best observed during a prolonged journey. Twice I have studied them, walking between Cornwall and Caithness. On my southward journey the crocus was flowering at Loch Lomond while daffodils faded from Falmouth. Mile after mile on the northward journey I saw what seemed to be the same hawthorn with its day-old foliage:

> To the delightful green
> Of you, fair radiant eyre. . . .

William Drummond's couplet goes to the root and also to the summit of the scene because the greenness of a leaf is conditioned by its amount of chlorophyll, which itself is conditioned by the amount of sunlight. Chlorophyll (so-named by two French chemists in 1817) nourishes a plant by absorbing carbon dioxide and by producing carbohydrates. The nature of that photosynthesis remains a mystery, but we do know that chlorophyll plays a vital part in it by transmuting the sun's radiant energy. At the other extreme, down in darkness, the root-hairs of a plant absorb from the soil a solution of food substances or sap which in April flows strongly, to be checked when September constricts the arteries.

April's change of scene is both restful and zestful, for of all colours green falls most gently on the retina, which is why we use it in our sun glasses. Mary Webb called it "the emblem of well-founded hope". "There are," she said, "a hundred shades of it in one field." Dryden preferred the oak, which he saluted as "the patriarch of trees". Cobbett chose the ash: "None," he declared, "equals it." To Eden Phillpotts an April larch shone "with emeralds of fire". Robert Nichols praised the poplar with its "silver leaves in sunny silence". Edward Thomas was a beech man; for him the leaves of that tree were "more aerial and pure and wild than birds". Green may indeed claim to be the colour of life because the word itself comes from the Old Teutonic *gro*, which was anglicised as 'grow'. We still use it to describe immaturity (there was a tautological teasing in the title of the Victorian novel about an undergraduate, *Verdant Green*). Life does not die with youth, neither is 'senile' a proper synonym for 'decay'; wherefore Charles Lamb remarked of a hale old man "He is yet in green and vigorous senility".

But green is only one segment of the April spectrum. Do you remember these lines by William Allingham?

> Four ducks on a pond,
> A grass-bank beyond.
> A blue sky of spring,
> White clouds on the wing;
> What a little thing
> To remember for years
> —To remember with tears.

I recall a similar experience while passing a meadow where lambs grazed among daffodils beneath cherry blossom. The meadow is scarcely a quarter-mile from the house, yet only once in thirty years have I seen lambs, daffodils, and blossom assembled there together.

This month the sounds change, too. Farmers stolid as oxen will halt when the first cuckoo calls; and I have overheard shepherds (alone, as they supposed, on the fells) answering the bird unashamedly. Swallows arrive, preparing to make a summer. All round the coast, and far inland on estuaries and rivers, men hammer happily at garboard or rudderpost, ready for the launching. Ploughing is over and done, but I was lately greeted by the jingle of a chain-harrow hauled by a Shire horse near Chipping Campden. Homeliest of all, lawn-mowers clatter from cottage gardens . . . not the mechanised mower, which disturbs half a parish, but the pushable mower, cheerful as corncrakes, and not loud enough to awaken the council roadman who rests like a crusador with a scythe at his feet.

Upon the other three seasons we bestow a neuter gender, or at most we allow that winter in a genial mood is He; but the fickle-fertile spring is a She whom G. M. Hopkins praised:

> Nothing is so beautiful as spring—
> When weeds, in wheels, shoot long and lovely and lush;
> Thrush's eggs look like little low heavens, and thrush
> Through the echoing timber does so wrinse and wring
> The ear, it strikes like lightnings to him sing. . . .

How swiftly we adapt ourselves to the change of scene; how

lightly we doff the wintry habits that so lately seemed eternal. Gazing at an empty hearth, we are surprised to remember the logs that warmed the winds of March. Deck chairs take the place of gumboots in the garden. Gloves, scarves, hotwater bottles, cough mixtures . . . all seem anachronisms. And is it possible that we really did carry a torch on our walk to the teatime post? Now we awake to the cuckoo; and at the end of the day, when we open the bedroom window to bid the world sleep well, a nightingale may sing Amen.

England's Birthday

The lanes of Warwickshire seemed even greener than on the morning when an unknown countryman first baptised them with that name. The River Stour lay like a blue thread, except when it entered a copse, and there it became a silver needle. Honington and Idlicote still cherished a house or two which Shakespeare may have seen when, as a truant schoolboy, he forgot his Latin and Greek, and learned instead the lessons that Ariel taught:

> Merrily, merrily, shall I live now
> Under the blossom that hangs on the bough.

It was good, I thought, in the youth of the year, to wander among scenes which Shakespeare's youth had known; and especially good to make such a pilgrimage at the season of the anniversary of his birth, 23rd April. And what happy chance, whereby the calendar has timed him to rhyme with England's patron saint.

If only because England falls short of their own national zeal, the rest of the kingdom will not resent this our celebration of a double English rubric. On the contrary, every true patriot must approve, knowing that no man can love his own land unless he respect another's. Without that respect he lapses into infatuation, the subtlest form of self-seeking. Many shrill voices assure us that to live for one's country is a naive and narrow ideal, and that to die for it is unforgiveable. Any scribbler is free to descant upon the 'futility' of war, yet feels no obligation to mention the fact that, if his fathers had not fought and won those wars, a large part of Europe would have sunk in a German ocean. But that is by the way.

My own way—which led to Whatcote—revealed some of the reasons why the English countryside is less collectively self-conscious than the other three kingdoms. For example, our own countryfolk never spoke a common medieval dialect or language. Their landscape, too, is more varied, and breeds a more varied type of man: Durham collier, Essex fowler, Cumbrian shepherd, Dean forester, Cockney lighterman, Shire grazier, Devon seadog. There is a sense in which a dalesman would die for Yorkshire, but might invite Sussex to fight its own battles. The English are more hybrid than the Gaels and Celts, and more likely to become more hybrid because they have foundered in an industrial Sargasso where pleasure and plenty sap the will to serve anything greater than themselves. Moreover the English are not only shy of their heritage; they indulge an unhistoric guilt toward it. We hear much from certain quarters about the nations whom England 'enslaved', but little about the roads, drains, schools, law courts, hospitals, and other amenities which marked the zenith of an empire that did more good and less harm than any other empire yet recorded. And would those 'slaves' have fared more comfortably under Russia? Or Japan? Or Germany? Or themselves? Nevertheless, the English continue to feel guilty and embarrassed. To the rest of this kingdom they do indeed owe an incalculable debt, yet the fact remains, by sheer weight of numbers their own prowess fore-ordained them to become the senior partner. Without England, for how long could the economy last? Twenty-four hours? Twenty-four days?

I lingered at Whatcote, watching the lambs that skipped and jumped. Times have changed since Shakespeare walked the green lanes of Warwickshire. But what *are* times, and do they really change beyond recognition? Carl Jung, who saw more deeply than most into our basic needs, loved not only his land but also his lineage. He was proud to blazon the family coat-of-arms: "A cross azure in chief dexter, and on base sinister a blue bunch of grapes on a field or. . . ." If one of the *tres magi* of modern psychology could feel such pride, then every Englishman stands four-square to all who mock his own pride. But that pride must be proper. Tottenham Hotspurs and the Corkscrewers Union are a poor substitute for England and St George. Not even a cut in the bank rate is quite so profoundly beneficial as a right use of the symbols of saintliness.

Shakespeare himself was an actor as well as a playwright. He must often have muttered: "Typical Monday night audience. Hard as nails, m'boy." If that audience had been likely to jeer, he would never have written:

> This happy breed of men, this little world . . .
> This blessed plot, this earth, this realm, this England.

Most of the "happy breed" were poor. They suffered what we now call social injustice. Yet those same men stood cheering and weeping when John of Gaunt raised himself from his deathbed to bless

> This land of such dear souls, this dear dear land,
> Dear for her reputation through the world.

The great mysteries of life, the so-called human predicament, do not change. Birth and death, love and hate, seedtime and harvest—those are the same as when Adam went forth from Eden. If therefore one generation shrinks from its predicament in anger and disillusion, while another generation shoulders it with faith and a sprinkle of good humour, then clearly the difference is to be explained not by the predicament but by the people.

Our fathers did not lie abed. They were up betimes. And in the evening of their life they said: "These wounds I had on Crispin's day." Like it or not, that is one reason why we are still able to battle for solvency as a nation whose imperial commitments end eastward of Clacton pier. There are no more worlds for England to conquer. She seems unwilling even to defend her green and pleasant land against the Philistines. Shakespeare was wiser than he knew when he mourned because

> England, that was wont to conquer others,
> Hath made a shameful conquest of itself.

If an Englishman would celebrate St George's Day, let him do so by resolving to detect and to oppose all who threaten the dwindling acres of rural England and their ways of life; for those ways and acres are something more than a pretty picture; they are a defence against starvation, thrombosis, and the intolerable tedium of nursemaiding a machine.

Next after Shakespeare stands Milton, who uttered a challenge which we must either answer or dismiss; "Lords and Commons of England, consider what Nation it is whereof ye are. . . ."

5

Spring Ancient and Modern

The surest way of assessing a nation is to savour its poetry, for that distils the attar of an era. Nowhere is this more evident than in our forefathers' praise of spring. The medieval lyricists amaze us as much by the number as by the ardour of their songs. One poet rejoices because "Lenten is come with love to town". Another says the same thing obliquely: "Winter wakeneth all my care." Chaucer opens his *Canterbury Tales* with a greeting to the April showers that bring forth May flowers:

> When that April with his showers soft
> The drought of March hath piercèd to the root. . . .

King James the First of Scotland aspires to sing like the birds (and he, too, bids winter a good riddance):

> Worship ye that love well this May,
> For of your bliss the Kalendis are begone,
> And sing with us, Away, Winter, away!

Reading such paeans, a modern countryman assumes that the world has lost its innocence and therewith the joy of life; yet he might well assume a second half-truth, that the world has lost its joy of life because it has gained the kingdom of comfort. Consider, for example, the lot of a mediaeval peasant. His home was a mud-and-wattle hut, scantily thatched, without windowpane or chimney pot. If he could find any, he burned damp logs in the middle of the floor, and their smoke wandered erratically through a hole in the roof. Only the rich could afford to buy candles; the rest fumbled by the glimmer of a reed dipped in grease. Many cottagers supped and slept within a few feet of their cow or their pig. Contrary to tradition, the wealthier classes washed themselves every day (some had a chair fixed in their tub); but the farmfolk seldom took a bath, and were strangers to a varied diet. Consider, too, the meagre winter diet. Most of the skinny stock was slaughtered during autumn because they had not yet learned to grow winter keep. Week after week, month by month, a noisome plate of salted meat was the staple diet of those who could procure it. If a peasant were caught poaching, it was no defence to plead that his family starved. The Forest Courts hanged him, or maimed him, or seized his stint of worldly goods. He might even be excommunicated. Nor did misery end with the Middle Ages; William Cowper told an eighteenth-century truth:

> The frugal housewife trembles when she lights
> Her scanty stock of brushwood. . . .

The longest hour of all—the hour before the dawn of spring— was the season of Lent and its abstinence from meat. The household of a fifteenth-century Earl of Leicester consumed one thousand salt herring every day throughout Lent. No wonder a medieval schoolboy wrote ruefully to his father: "Thou wyll not beleve how wery I am off fyshe, and how moch I desir that flesh were cum in ageyn, for I have ate non other but salt fysh this Lent. . . ." Three centuries later, another Earl of Leicester showed England how to improve its winter keep, but the good news spread (so he reckoned) at the rate of one mile a year; such was the conservatism of Norfolk farmers. And again the misery did not end with the Middle Ages. Except for the acquisition of window-panes and chimney pots, an Irish farmhand at the beginning of the last century fared as harshly as his ancestor under Gloriana.

Our own welcome to spring is chiefly aesthetic. The birds and the blossom make an agreeable change from central heating and electric blankets. But the older welcome was more eloquent, more ardent, because spring really did mean the end of long nights, shivering dawns, smoke-smarting eyes, and winter's iron ration. The ardent eloquence was not a prerogative of poets. All men shared it—even the austere Fathers, stooping in a draughty scriptorium. Gregory of Nyssa chose the springtime for his text:

"The sadness of winter has passed, and with it the unpleasant rains . . . the meadows are filled with flowers . . . the fig tree is putting forth its fruit, and the vine is blossoming." You find the same jubilation among the chroniclers. Bede, for instance, prefaced his *History* with some remarks about the English climate; but a modern Regius Professor would hardly add a footnote to say that the sun was shining, that his study no longer leaked, and that he had enjoyed green peas for luncheon.

Spring, in short, is not what it used to be, because we ourselves have half-tamed the winter. Cowper's "frugal housewife" no longer crouches before a few twigs on the hearth. Schoolboys no longer eat rank herrings. Both for better and for worse we are our brothers' and our sisters' keeper; and never before has English poetry been so stubbornly down in the dumps. How remarkable, therefore—how inexplicable by Marxist fallacies—were the courage and gaiety of those faraway ill-fed countryfolk who, having emerged from winter's tomb, beat their fist gladly upon the womb of spring:

> Spring, the sweet spring, is the year's pleasant king;
> Then blooms each thing, then maids dance in a ring;
> Cold doth not sting, the pretty birds do sing. . . .

So sang Thomas Nashe.

> Sweet air, blow soft; mount, lark, aloft,
> To bid my love good morrow.

So sang Thomas Heywood; and Carew said Amen:

> The valleys, hills, and woods in rich array
> Welcome the coming of the long'd for May.

Such plain living evoked a singing so high that few now could pitch their own powers against it. Not even the late Mr T. S. Eliot touched quite the same chord as that with which old William Browne bade Shepherd Roget to pull his socks up:

> Roget, droop not, see the spring
> Is the earth enamelling,
> And the birds in every tree
> Greet this morn with melody. . . .

That is the voice of the wind on the heath, of the beck through the fells, the bird from the bough, the song in the heart.

The Voice of the People

There are several ways of gauging public opinion. One is to gallop through a region, asking a few questions (we call it the scientific method); another is to move leisurely through a region, answering many questions (we call that the intuitive method). Now to go from door to door is a form of intrusion to which I could not easily submit myself, not even although I received a bonus on every vacuum cleaner so disposed of. What I can do, and have spent my life doing, is to wander aimfully throughout rural Britain, minding other people's business by listening to the postman, talking with the laird, and overhearing a publican. Wordsworth described such conversations as

> the talk
> Man holds with weekday man in the hourly walk
> Of the mind's business. . . .

In my callow or student days I made the Fabian's arrogant mistake of supposing that only a bookish élite can be usefully questioned: *vox populi vox diaboli*. To consult shepherds and ploughmen on Votes for Murderers was, I assumed, a mutual waste of time. Such men had not read the statistics. After a while, however, I became conscious that ploughmen and shepherds were often more sceptical and less dogmatic than many so-called objective scientists. Clearly, it is idle to discuss India with a man who has never heard of the Upanishads; but when the issue comes nearer home, then neither A nor O has any necessary connection with the level of common sense. For example, which is the more deterring—to be hanged forever, or to be comfortably confined until you are thirty-five? Has England the right to remain English, or must she learn to speak European, and, like Rome in decline, import aliens for her dreary work? Until television has elected our first President, ought not the Queen to be addressed, not as the Head of a State, but as Box C3, c/o World Government? Questions of that kind require more than an average understanding of human dynamics (one's own included). Sometimes they seem so painful that we prefer not to answer (nor even to ask) them.

In what follows I shall try to speak for the majority of country-folk whose voices I have heard. My own voice, occasionally my own views, are not the same as theirs, or at any rate are sufficiently different to deserve redefinition. But I am not discussing my own views. I am recording other people's. Thus, even in the most unlikely places—a Cornish shipyard, perhaps—you may hear the voice of the people discussing foreign policy: "I served there six years with my regiment. Maybe they didn't have a vote. Maybe they couldn't read the bloody vote-paper anyway. But I'll tell 'ee one thing . . . the poor bastards wasn't killing each other with British tanks and Bolshey aircraft."

In Wensleydale they can express both sides of a question: "Now shut thy gabble, and listen. Suppose 'twas like England today . . . too many people and not enough space. Dost think they'd allow white men in, thousands and thousands every year? Dost think . . . nay, shut up and listen for a change . . . dost think Mrs Nehru would ask her taxpayers to build new schools so's English kids could learn the lingo? Dost think yon Colonel Bomba would pass a law agin advertising for a Bombanese boilermaker?"

Occasionally our fellowcountrymen speak so plainly that we flinch from their truthfulness: "All right, then. Foreigners are 'uman beings, same as we are. Kick us and we cry. Tickle and we laugh. But just answer me something. Plain yes or no. Dost fancy thy Jane walking out wi' one on 'em?" Silence. "Aye, and there's summat else . . . do they like to see one o' their lasses walking out wi' our lads?" Nobody ventures a pseudo-Freudian *tu quoque*. "I'll tell thee what is agin the rights of man, and that's to send kindly folks from their native land, to sit and shiver in't fog."

The Welsh farmwife is another who speaks for the majority: "Whenever they hanged a murderer, there was always a crowd outside the jail, carrying placards of sympathy. Do they take their sympathy to the widow's house? And don't talk to me about statistics, man. They only show how many people haven't been deterred by jail. What I'd like to know is how many millions *were* deterred by hanging."

Most villagers stand against the Common Market. Again I am not examining the validity of their arguments. All I seek to show is the force with which those arguments are expressed: "Oi don't see why 'tis always us must change our ways. 'Ave you ever met a Frenchie as warnted to swap 'is decimal for an 'alf-crown? Or a

Jerry as warnted to steer on our soide o' the road? Thirty year ago we was English, and doing all roight considering. So wart's 'appened, eh? Wart's 'appened?"

Coleridge asked that question in 1830, and then answered it: "The stock-jobbing and moneyed interest is so strong in this country, that it has more than once prevailed in our foreign councils over national honour and national justice." Despite a preoccupation with opium and German metaphysics, Coleridge kept his ear to the ground, knowing that the battle must be long and bitter; knowing also that not even Canning, the Prime Minister, could stop the rot: "The country gentlemen are not slow to join the foreign influence. Canning felt this very deeply, and said he was unable to contend with the city trained bands."

When the Palace of Westminster (or Houses of Parliament) was burned down in 1834 many Londoners wished to see it re-built in the Green Park. But the Duke of Wellington insisted that MPs ought not to be placed in a position so easily accessible to the mob. In other words, our downtrodden fathers really did exert some influence over their lords and masters. Today our violence is reserved for spoil-sport occasions, and we listen meekly while MPs debate whether some subversive Briton has breached their wellpaid privileges. A majority of those same members assure us that their wisdom and understanding so far excel our own that we must submit to be led by them out of the errors of our ways. And led we are, by the nose. In the course of a long history the British people have accepted hundreds of unpopular laws, but never before have so many members of both Houses defied so many demands by so many voters.

Postman's Knock

"The postman," said Voltaire, "consoles life." And Thackeray added: "Blessed is he who is made happy by the sound of a rat-tat." To most people nowadays Postman's Knock is simply the name of a coy pursuit that was indulged at their grandparents' inhibited soirées. The Royal Mail slips through our letter-box silently unannounced. A shop steward, no doubt, could compute the number of working hours that are 'saved' by postmen who no longer lift a hand to help us. But there are exceptions to that rule and indeed to several others which depict modern postmen as inaudible automata. In Monmouthshire I was startled by what seemed to be three rifle shots, followed by the sound of breaking glass and a shrill voice: "Evans Post, there's no need to be supersonic, surely," to which the Post replied: "Missus, that old Crystal Palace was due to come down with the walls of Jericho." Yes, you are right: the front door contained a stained-glass panel, and the postman's knock had shattered it.

It is surprising how variously our country posts arrive. When I am living on Exmoor my letters are delivered from a motor-cycle and sometimes on foot. In the Chilterns they come by car. In Wales they may ride a pony through the snow. Piel Island, off the Lancashire coast, receives its Final Demand by punt.

Where, then, is Britain's most arduous postal round? I can cite one candidate that might take first prize. It lies in the wildest part of West Wales; and there, when I was starting to plough, the postman arrived, pushing his bicycle. An hour later, when I stopped the tractor, the postman departed, having refreshed himself with coffee in the kitchen. And if ever a man deserved to rest, it was that traveller, for he had trundled his machine nearly two thousand feet into the air, opening and shutting twelve gates while he climbed a track which in southern England would be called a rutted rut. When snow fell it was a whole day's work for him to reach the farm: "There's times I've been there with only an old Pools paper to deliver. Ah, and I've had to deliver it even when I've known they were all away to Aberystwyth. I took a turkey up there once. Seven days after Christmas. There was a rail strike. I've been off turkey ever since."

The Scots, they say, have the second sight; but that Welsh postman possessed a third ear. One night, for instance, the farmer undertook a journey which, for properly private reasons, he wished to keep secret. He set out at 2 a.m., along by-lanes, driving fast without stopping. On his return he was astonished when the postman said: "You had a good trip to Cardigan last night, I shouldn't wonder?" It is possible that the postman had shared the secret extrasensorily: but in my opinion he got it from someone who saw somebody who met another body who recognised the farmer's car speeding through moonlit Lampeter. In either case the mystery was stated by Wordsworth:

> there is a dark
> Inscrutable workmanship. . . .

I used to visit one of the most isolated farms within forty miles of London, at a time when farms within forty miles of London really could be isolated. The place stood on a hill at the end of a mile-long track. The farmer seldom wrote, and more rarely replied, partly from inclination and partly because agriculture was not then conducted via a nationalised correspondence course. One letter weekly seemed a fair average for Solitary Farm. The local postmaster was therefore puzzled when one of his postmen took to visiting the farm every day. Many years later the postman himself explained to me the reason for those regular visits to a remote and hitherto uncommunicative place: "Oi was courting th' old gaffer's daughter, see? And oi said to her, 'Margy,' oi said, 'reckon oi could 'ave a meal 'ere every day if oi was to wroite.' So oi did. And then, o' course, oi 'ad to deliver it."

"Did you," I asked, "write long letters?"

"Not me," he replied, "Oi just wrote wart oi fancied for dinner." Less laconic was the rural Valentine which Margaret Brews sent to her future husband, John Paston of Norfolk, in February 1477: "Right reverend and worshipful and my right well-beloved Valentine, I recommend me unto you most heartily, desiring to hear of your welfare, which I beseech Almighty God long for to preserve unto his pleasure and your heart's desire." And because the young man was far away, the girl confessed "this letter was indite with full heavy heart, By your own MB". That, of course, was written in the years before 'professional' women indulged motherhood as a part-time hobby.

The foundations of our country post were laid by Ralph Allen whom Fielding depicted as Squire Allworthy, "intrinsically rich and noble, without tinsel, or external Ostentation". Allen had begun his postal career as mail-sorter and errand boy, at a time when the deputy-postmaster at Bath received ten shillings a week, and the average country postmaster was a publican or some other kind of village tradesman. By his own private enterprise Allen bequeathed to the kingdom a complex yet efficient system of cross-country deliveries. Not every city approved the bequest. Wells, for instance, refused to "suffer the Riders to blow their Hornes as they ride through . . .". If a delay did occur, it was ascribed rather to individuals than to the system. In 1797 a warning went out to the Hereford and Worcester Mailcoach: "If any Post-Boy or Rider, carrying this Mail, is found to loiter on the Road, he will be committed to a House of Correction, and confined to hard labour for one Month." As a result, the post-boys (some of them were girls) rode so furiously that the local gentry denounced them as Jehus. One wonders what Ralph Allen would have said to the present Post Office, which delivers no morning mail at all to parts of Buckinghamshire.

There is one postal service that never will be seen again; and the other day my father recalled it for me—his delight, as a child, in watching the lamps of the mail-carts weaving like glow-worms through Cornish lanes to catch the night train.

In Search of Paradise

Lost in a maze of lanes, I met a villager to whom I showed a map which the estate agent had drawn.

"I know where the house is," the villager said, "but I don't know whether you'll ever find it." Then he pointed over his shoulder. "You follow that lane, and bear right and left. And then you turn left. You'd better watch out 'cause there's cows. There's a cross-roads next, just by a farm, and there you turn right. Then presently you'll reach a hill that goes down a bit. But don't *you* go down or you won't never git nowhere. Anyway, just where it goes down, you'll see a cart-track. It's up there."

It was indeed, and all paradise with it; a little house of warm red brick and steeply sloping roof, with a tiny garden from which you stepped straight into meadows that dipped out of sight and then swept up again, two miles away, to reach a white-washed church. It did not matter that the house lacked a telephone and electricity. Nor did it matter that no newspaper was delivered, no bread, no meat. What did matter was the vista, the stillness, the knowledge that distance made the place inviolate. Even before I had unlocked the front door, I said: "This is where I will live, and this where I shall die."

That was thirty-three years ago, in what now seems another world, from which no man could have foretold that bungalows would be dumped where cows had grazed; that breeches and leggings would evoke a giggle; that someone would telephone the police when she saw a gamekeeper carrying his gun through the village. Thus it came to pass that paradise was lost, and I found myself cast forth from Eden, self-exiled in search of paradise regained. But where to begin that search? Suddenly I remembered Clough's vision—"Westward, look, the land is bright." Westward lay Exmoor, the land of my mothers. So away I went, a shade slower perhaps, but scarcely less hopeful, than on that spring morning when the villager pointed the way.

My reception on Exmoor was what the hotels call H and C. The C or cold occurred when I overheard a farmer explaining how he had caused the cost of living: "I paid two hundred pounds for it. That was in 1940. And for near thirty years I let it at ten bob a week. So what's that? Call it seven hundred. And t'other day I sold it for three thousand. So that's three thousand, five hundred profit, less fifty for slapping a pint o' paint on now and again. Easy money, eh?"

However, things warmed-up when I got talking with a man from Bampton, where they hold the Exmoor pony sales.

"Davey?" he echoed. "Your great-great-grandfather? My dear soul, he were vicar o' Bampton were old Bart Davey. A praper fox-hunting gent. But a good pa'son, mind." He scratched his ear. "Lord, Lord, that's a time ago, surely?"

"Two hundred years," I said.

"Still, Davey's a real Devon name. We'm all Devon down yere. And that's how we aim to keep it. So you shouldn't have no difficulty in finding a cottage. Not if your grand-greatest were old Bartholomew Davey."

Alas, neither privilege nor piety are what they used to be. The Exmoor estate agents showed no interest at all in the Rev. Bart Davey, M.A., of Blundell's and Balliol (and of King's College, Cambridge, also) vicar of Bampton two centuries ago. Fortunately, I soon regained a glimpse of paradise. It stood about a mile beyond a moorland village, on a hill yet in a hollow, and was shielded by trees. I arrived via a track that branched from one of those happy lanes whereon grass grows like a parting down the middle, and the steep Maytime banks resemble a florist's shop alight with primroses. As though to ensure privacy, a signpost at the head of the lane said "Unsuitable For Motors". Alas again, the price was beyond my prospects; and I felt no ambition to celebrate my centenary by remarking: "Only another ten years, and the house will be mine."

Soon after that I heard of a remote cottage on the fringe of the moor, almost within sight of the sea. But once again it was not to be, for my investigation ended when the owner said indignantly: "Roof? Now look yere, mister, I never said the place had a roof. All I said was, it needs attention."

Then for a third time paradise appeared, when an agent sent news of a cottage "with all main conveniences, &c., and garage, standing alone in large garden, three miles from the village." I blinked at the price, £2,950. If I rifled the piggy bank, I could sidestep a bridging loan. That very morning I went to have a look. The cottage was exactly as the agent described it. The only thing he had omitted to mention was the din from summer motorists on a main road ten yards away.

And so it went on. Day after day I sighted paradise, and always it was either not for sale or in some other way unsuitable. Moreover, I wished to live in the Devon sector of Exmoor, a relatively small region with far fewer houses than Somerset possessed. But I refused to give up. Exmoor, after all, was my homeland *de jure* because of old Bart Davey, and *de facto* because I had long since learned and loved it. In the end the search became morbid. Whenever I passed a secluded cottage, I found myself peering over the garden wall—even through the kitchen window—computing whether the occupants were likely to die before I did.

Then at last paradise really was regained, or at any rate demiparadise. Having heard of my search, a friend led me to a one-room residence on his estate, at the edge of a wood, up the steepest lane I ever climbed. The Severn Sea lay twelve minutes' walk from the door. Two arcs of Exmoor rose like a wind-shield. Day and night a stream sang within a yard of the window. Said my friend: "It's all yours." It was indeed. In it and around it I found places and people who, instead of falling face-flatward into futurity, have the wit to blend the best of the past and of the present. One room, however, seems considerably less than two; therefore the search continued; and I confess there were times when I put a sombre interpretation on that faraway villager's warning: "I don't know whether you'll ever find it."

After two more years I did find it. But that must be another story.

Nocturne

"I have been one acquainted with the night." So said Robert Frost, who, being a farmer as well as a poet, understood that night life in the country is not at all the same as night life in a town.

For most villagers closing-time means bedtime. The land, after all, awakes early, and men who live by it may not lie abed. Farmers would soon be bankrupt if they tied themselves to a forty-hour week. That—and not a scarcity of entertainment—is the chief reason why lights in the countryside go out early. In the old times, of course, they went out even earlier. Men laboured then from sunrise till sunset, and their only machines were a horse and an ox and a plough. All else was manual work, done against the clock and sometimes against a threat of famine. Like the birds, our forbears lay down with the sun. Yet even in the old times there were men who knew the night; poaching men, capaciously pocketed; or the guard of the Royal Mail, with his ears and maybe a blunderbuss cocked while the smoking horses halted for an instant on the summit; or shepherds watching over their flocks. The heirs of such men still see night life in the country, albeit their observations are made in the course of prosaic duty.

Others have loved the night for its own sake. Dorothy Wordsworth's *Journal* is full of starry exploits. During the spring of 1802 she noted that Wordsworth composed a nocturne: "He walked on our path and wrote the lines; he called me into the orchard, and there he repeated them to me. He stayed there till eleven o'clock." On another spring night—the first of May—Wordsworth composed another poem: "Three solitary stars in the middle of the blue vault," Dorothy remembered, "and one or two on the points of the high hills. William wrote *The Celandine* tonight."

> Pleasures newly-found are sweet
> When they lie about our feet.

And Dorothy ended with a poem of her own, in prose: "Heard the cuckoo tonight, the first of May."

A few people still enjoy comparable adventures. For several years I shared a nightly walk with two friends whose work kept them indoors all day. During our journeys we would overhear a rabbit rustling the frozen grass; we would identify (if we could) a shrill bird's cry among the beeches; we would watch a fieldmouse moving leisurely through moonbeams on the lane; and when the nightingale sang, we remembered that Milton, too, had listened:

> Thy liquid notes that close the eye of Day. . . .

Naturalists may protest that the best season for such things is winter when the nights are long. Even so, there is a magic in the brevity of these near-summer nights, which makes us forget that we have not been to bed. On Exmoor there were rifts of daylight within an hour of midnight, and a moon so bright that I could read the inscription on Dunkery plinth. Everywhere the night life announced itself with creepings and hootings and bleatings. Twice a vixen barked, fifty yards from Oare church; and on the road to Simonsbath—in the very middle of the road—a deer was taking the air. Far out across the Severn Sea, the port-light of a steamer shone like a ruby in a silver salver cast by the moon.

Sleepless as an owl, the lighthouse lowered and raised its punctual eyelid. Streams tinkled, invisible through the heather; and when a stray breeze stirred, it was as though the universe had sighed, thereby breaking the rule which Robert Nichols detected when he paused

> To feel the world, tilted on axle-tree,
> In slow gyration, with no sensible sound. . . .

Few people would choose to camp under a frozen hedge, but if

you have ever slept out of doors in May you will agree with
Stevenson when he said: "Night is a monotonous period under a
roof; but in the open world it passes lightly, with its stars and
dews and perfumes; and the hours are marked by changes in the
face of Nature. What seems a kind of temporal death to people
choked between walls and curtains, is only a light and living
slumber to the man who sleeps afield." Stevenson noted also the
hour before dawn: "It is then that the cock first crows, not this
time to announce the dawn, but like a cheerful watchman speeding
the night." The animals respond to that emanation, though no
one can explain it. "Even shepherds," said Stevenson, "have not a
guess as to the means or purpose of this nightly resurrection.
Towards two in the morning they declare the thing takes place;
and neither know nor enquire further." Shakespeare knew the
hour, for then the ghost of Hamlet's father stalked the ramparts:
"It was about to speak when the cock crew."

Meanwhile, even at three o'clock, a light shone in darkness, and
I guessed that the shepherd was lacing his boots, ready for some
arduous work with a Border collie. Once I passed a motor-
cyclist who (if I recognised him aright) was away to collect the
milk-lorry. So swiftly the time sped, so intent the watching and
listening, I was surprised when a tree seemed to move toward me.
But it was not the tree that moved; it was the Earth, approaching
what we call sunrise. Slowly the stars slipped, and the darkness
dwindled. Soon after three o'clock a lark sprang up, spilling his
song like minims of joy. Within half an hour every combe and
every summit was echoing its own dawn chorus, as it were citing
chapter and verse for C. Day Lewis:

> Cease denying, begin knowing.
> Comes peace this way here, comes renewing
> With down of bird and bud. . . .

May's sleepless nights are never exhausting. When the sun does
appear, it bathes all tiredness from your eyes. At noon, perhaps,
you begin to feel drowsy, but pleasantly so; and at nine o'clock
you re-live your childhood by going to bed while the sun is still
up. You fall asleep at once, untroubled by thoughts of getting and
spending. Pleasant memories croon their own lullaby:

> I have been one acquainted with the night.
> I have outwalked the city's furthest light.

An English Heritage

While re-exploring the Lincolnshire Wolds I visited an old
acquaintance at Caistor; not a human being but a grammar school.
Alongside some modern additions, the original building—of
reddish ironstone—is well-preserved and actively employed. Its
doorway utters a silent boast: 1631. There Sir Henry Newbolt
acquired a culture whose best-known harvest is *Drake's Drum*:

> Drake He's in his hammock till the great Armadas come.
> (Capten, art tha sleepin' there below?)

Every countryman knows that the grammar schools are not and
never were a privilege of the few. As G. M. Trevelyan said, they
served and still do serve "the relatively poor, the lower middle class,
and the sons of minor gentry, yeomen, burghers". Yet the grammar schools are now a target for the malice of State monopolists.

Have those monopolists never ventured beyond their own
parish? Is their malice so vicious that it can distort the facts by
creating a fantasy wherein every grammar school is a luxurious
hothouse for the breeding of polo players? Let the monopolist
visit Kirkby Lonsdale Grammar School, where one aristocrat will
shout to another: "Thee's nobbut a neet-weet." Let him visit
Barnstaple, where the gilded youths remark of their paternal
acres: "Us be a-shearing come Monday."

I am not myself an Old Grammarian grinding his nostalgic axe.
It so happens that I received the inestimable blessing of a classical
education at one of our ancient public schools; and there I studied
the long and honourable lineage of grammar schools, and came to
understand that they were made-to-measure for boys whose talents
transcend a State school, but whose aspirations fall short of a
Sherborne or a Shrewsbury.

Consider Dent Grammar School in the West Riding of Yorkshire; a building so small that it would scarcely serve as village
hall. During the eighteenth century a Dent lad was educated there,
Adam Sedgwick, who became Professor of Geology at Cambridge. The school itself was closed seventy years ago, but Dent
Town still tends it as an historic monument. Consider St Albans
Grammar School, which taught Nicholas Breakspear, better-

known as Adrian IV, the only Englishman who became Pope. Consider Hull Grammar School, the "kindly nurse" of Andrew Marvell and William Wilberforce. Consider Grantham Grammar School; in 1645 one of its pupils answered to the name of Newton, and today we respond by calling him Sir Isaac. If the grammar schools made a roll-call of the great, many ghosts would answer *Adsum*. Queen Elizabeth's Treasurer, Lord Burghley, was a grammar school boy; so also were Bishop Jewel, Francis Bacon, John Gay, John Vanburgh, William Wordsworth, Thomas de Quincey, W. E. Henley, Graham Greene, Edward Heath.

At those schools a cross-section of rural society scanned its way among dactyls and spondees. In 1759 one of the pupils at Beverley Grammar School was the son of a cobbler; another was the son of Lord Elibank. In 1800 the poor scholars at Bury Grammar School were winning exhibitions to Brasenose College, Oxford, and to St John's College, Cambridge. In 1868 the grammar school at Worcester had achieved such distinction that Queen Victoria dubbed it Royal. Harrow and Bedford are only two of several schools which dropped their syntactical style, and became public schools, basking in famous glory. The country grammar school, by contrast, remains well-content with a roll-call of craftsmen, councillors, doctors, parsons, lawyers, and those farmers who raise a good crop and a happy family.

Even the humblest grammar school had something good to say of itself, as for example Tuxford, whose tale seems worth telling. On 30th July 1669, Charles Read, "beinge at this present something indisposed, but of sound and perfect minde and memory", bequeathed a sum of money wherewith to build and endow schools at Drax in Yorkshire, at Corby in Lincolnshire, and at Tuxford in Nottinghamshire. The Tuxford school was concerned with "the teaching of the youth and children of the inhabitants to read, write, cast accounts, and further instruct them in Latin as the occasion requires". Its founder stated: "I do ordain that four sons of widows of ministers and of decayed gentlemen and their widows who are not able to maintain their charge, shall have and be paid £5 per annum apiece." The pupils themselves performed tasks that would nowadays cause a strike: "I do ordain," said the founder, "that every one of the said boys shall by turns every Saturday in the afternoon, sweep and cleanse the said schoolhouse." The governors of Tuxford Grammar School were local worthies, "six able freeholders or others, men of integrity". At least one Old Boy became eminent—Walter Taylor, sometime Regius Professor of Greek at Cambridge. A century ago the master received a stipend of forty pounds a year, having then forty pupils at the school, not one of whom paid a penny for his education. Although Tuxford Grammar School was closed in 1915, its handsome building continues to serve as a centre for many kinds of civic activity.

A modern Philistine mocks the grammar schools because they taught Latin. But his mockery misses even the point of its own commercial astigmatism. Long after the Middle Ages, Latin survived as the Esperanto of educated Christendom. No man could enter any of the learned professions unless he were a passable Latinist. Even today a doctor must be able to tell the difference between *Papaver rhoeas* and *Atropa belladonna*. And if the Philistine himself learned Latin, he might avoid those caricatures of it which he indulges during moments of hollow orotundity.

The grammar schools of England were, and ought always to remain, among the glories of England. Their enemies have no other weapon than envy and deceit. But all will be lost if their defenders decline to answer back, for there are times when one must ascend to the level of the gallery, not in order to return its abuse, but rather to speak aloud and clear, as follows: every countryman knows that hundreds of thousands of parents could afford the modest fee of a grammar school if only they would slacken the speed at which they are now driving, drinking, gambling, and smoking themselves into a disgruntled grave.

6

Haytime

Haytime is a long time. In most parts of England they finish mowing in June, but in some parts of Scotland they do not begin until July. Britain rings the changes on a topographical tune:

> In Cambridgeshire forward to Lincolnshire way,
> The champion maketh his fallow in May.

That was Thomas Tusser in his *Five Hundred Good Points of Husbandry*. Shakespeare sounded even more succinct: "Ripeness is all." A farmer, however, cannot make hay simply because the sun happens to be shining. His crop must be gathered when it is ready, neither before nor after; and the readiness does not always coincide with a dry spell. The moment of mowing and the quality of the yield are conditioned by the autumn rains, the winter frost, and spring's uncertain wind. Like many other novices I used to despair of ever acquiring the magical expertise which knows when a meadow is ready. I never did pass beyond a novitiate, but at least I discarded the illusion of magic. Hay must be cut when most of the grasses are coming to flower, before the grain ripens—that is, before the food in each stem has moved upward to nourish the maturing seed.

Many townsfolk regard the hay crop as a pageant which farmers maintain for old time's sake—a kind of ritualistic lawn-mowing—but the farmers themselves do not share that view. To them a hayfield is so many trusses and loads and tons, to be translated as pounds, shillings, pence. I can still repeat a parrot-cry that was learned in the days of my farm pupilage: one truss of hay weighs half-a-hundredweight; thirty-six trusses make one load; therefore one load weighs nearly a ton. A typical meadow grass contains about 18 per cent moisture; 36 per cent digestible fibre, sugar, starch; and 6 per cent minerals, chiefly ash. There are 4,500 species of the *Gramineae* or grass family, but only a handful yield a good crop of hay. Their names, however, ring a pleasant bell: timothy, wavy hair, sheep's fescue, Yorkshire fog.

It is often said that technology has robbed haytime of its fragrance and its pageantry. Instead of a sweet smell, the fumes of a tractor rise above the swathes; and the phalanx of singing scythesmen has itself been mown-down by a regiment of reapers. On small farms, however, where the crop is turned and stacked by hand, the lavender-like loveliness still weaves its ancient spell, distilled from a substance called coumarin. The species *Anthoxanthum odoratum* is especially rich in coumarin, whence its everyday name, sweet vernal grass. The crop makes poor hay, but proffers the delicate nosegay which W. H. Hudson loved: "Is there," he asked, "a man on earth in such despair, so overloaded with cares and maddened with anxious thought, who would not find instant relief and forgetfulness of all his miseries on inhaling this delicious fragrance?"

Driving across Salisbury Plain while the machines disgorge their bales, a townsman may suppose that Progress has at last compelled the farmers to face reality. But one man's realism may be another's ruin. In remote parts of Britain you can still see "the tawny mowers" whom Marvell watched in Wharfedale three centuries ago, swinging their sibilant scythes. Skilled haytimers cherished those scythes, as a cricketer now cherishes his bat, or a violinist his Stradivarius; not for sentiment's sake, but because the implement symbolises and also secures a livelihood. Not a great while ago a Westmorland man told me that his father's scythe— the family bread-winner—was kept always in the parents' bedroom; and woe indeed to any who touched the protective sacking. It used to be said that a good worker could scythe four acres of barley in ten hours. I have met farmers who in their childhood saw twenty-five scythers reap twenty-five acres of barley between six o'clock and noon.

In Perthshire recently I walked beside a horse-drawn mower: "It was a birthday present," the farmer told me, "from my grannie." Then he scratched his nape. "Must be forty years since she passed on. But it's all I need. Anyway, I've no' the cash to buy a toy that'd work twelve hours a year."

"And the horse?" I asked.

"You can see for yourself. Bonnie as the day she was born."

"Fifteen years ago?"

"Fifteen? Mon, that's flattery. She came of age last week."

Down in Norfolk—near a farm which Rider Haggard once owned—a smallholder was scything his patch.

"Hard work," I observed.

"Very," came the reply. "But you'd have to pay a fiver for this amount of hay. And even then it might make thistle soup."

You will notice, by the way, that those old-time haymakers do not toss their swathes negligently. They turn them lightly so that sun and wind will drain the unwanted water, for grasses are covered with a film of waterproof wax which, if it is damaged, may allow moisture to seep through and remove the soluble nourishment. As for the hayrick, only science and craftsmanship can build aright. If the temperature of the rick exceeds 150° F. a gas (acetic aldehyde) will certainly spoil the crop, and may burn it.

Haytime or haysel is no longer a country festival. On the few farms which do maintain some of the pleasantries, the younger hands will forego the fun rather than miss their television. Yet one needs not be wholly a dotard in order to remember the time when some sort of festivity was still the rule. Happy ways, happy days; how often have I toiled in the sun, turning the swathes; how often have I lazed in the shade, sipping tea while one chiffchaff stirred the summer silence, and was drowned when the farmer's children came loping and laughing with fresh tea and more cakes and another rake. Was it business or was it pleasure? It was each, and yet it was more than both. Vergil defined it in three words: "O fortunate farmers!"

Lords of the Manor

All the world, they say, loves a lord; which is one reason why the world continues to buy lordships of the manor. Some purchasers, indeed, believe that by acquiring a lordship they will become peers of the realm. A manor, however, confers no such precedence; nor is the cost of its purchase likely to be off-set by any brand of businessmanship.

What, then, are the privileges of a lord of the manor? When and why were they conferred? A full answer to those questions would require a history of the feudal system; a short answer, even although it must sound superficial, is part of a proper understanding of the English countryside. Thus, when the Romans finally left Britain, the natives found little joy in their so-called independence. Men who had shouted "Romans go home!" were either killed or starved by the chaos which occurred when the Romans did go home. We are witnessing the same sort of liberty elsewhere today: the wars of rival gods, the feuds of ambitious leaders, the collapse of law and order. Bede's *History* proves how traumatic was the birth of the English people. Out of that anguish arose chieftains who offered security to the masses; and it is important to remember that the chieftain fulfilled an economic need. His style—'lord'—was an abbreviation of the Anglo-Saxon *hlaford*, one who provides *hlaf* or a loaf of bread. So, when the Normans arrived they had only to extend and as it were codify an established system. Both in theory and in practice all land belonged to the king, who, in return for military service, granted many manors to a few barons (but was careful so to scatter those manors that only a handful of friends were entrusted with a single vast estate). Inevitably the word 'manor' has been debased. William Morris, for example, bought and restored Kelmscot Manor beside the Thames near Lechlade; but his house had been built for a yeoman, and never was a manor. Sometimes the style is assumed so wildly that it becomes ludicrous, as at Great Missenden, where a licensed restaurant calls itself Chiltern Manor.

By a process known as sub-infeudation the barons granted smaller estates to lesser men, the typical lords of the manor, who nevertheless acknowledged the king to be their ultimate master. In his heyday the mediaeval lord presided over local courts, not as judge and jury, but as moderator. The Baron and the Customary Courts, for instance, dealt with civil disputes; the Court Leet, with minor crimes. Henry II and his successors modified and at length abolished the local assemblies; and in course of time the lords exchanged their medieval status for the role of country gentry, Justices of the Peace, holders maybe of an advowson. The best types of squire was symbolised by Sir Roger de Coverley, of whom Steele remarked: "His tenants grow rich, his servants look satisfied, all the young women profess to love him, and the young men are glad of his company." Sir Roger was not the product of sentimental fantasy. He was an amalgam of men so immediately recognisable as 'real' that he was accepted by the sophisticated readers for whose entertainment he had been devised. Not every squire was a gout-ridden magistrate who hunted six days a week, and spent the seventh compiling a list of starving labourers to be transported for poaching a pheasant.

What, then, remains to a modern lord of the manor? The answer lies midway between 'almost nothing' and 'less than nothing'. In 1922 the Law of Property Act reduced the lord of the manor to a picturesque anachronism. Even the reservation of mineral rights was stolen from him. Today, as a landowner, he is weighed down by all manner of obligations to a State intent upon destroying him by means of taxation. Having long ago ceased to provide bread, some lords of the manor would now be happy to receive a loaf.

The word 'manor' is Latin—*maneo* or 'I remain'—and the system itself suited an era of what Gilbert White called "stationary men". It is therefore idle to mourn the passing of an institution whose function no longer exists. But it is not at all idle to mourn the passing of a person who, at his best, gave to the village an identity, for lack of which the countryside has grown lonely and bewildered. Townsfolk never did feel the same need of a patron. They looked rather to the guilds, councils, trades unions.

A vicar is no substitute for the squire. His writ runs only among the few, and was not designed to encompass secular affairs. Nor can a parish council fill the gap; the butcher, the baker, and the worthy candlestickmaker may indeed lay down the law, or at any rate uphold it; but they never will enlist a personal allegiance. Who else remains? The local rich man? Very likely he owns a factory or some other business, and is seen only at weekends. He may do much good, and be well-liked, but he was not born to the manor. A true 'progressive' must therefore hope that the *novi homines* will maintain an ancient English tradition whereby the old landed gentry married into the new commercial interest, and so begat the best of both breeds.

A wayfarer in England soon learns to sift the shepherded from the leaderless village. Sometimes the difference can be detected at a glance; the cottages are cared for; the street is tidy; and no garage competes with a similar eyesore across the way. I think of Tissington in Derbyshire, which has been held by the FitzHerberts for centuries; of Honington in Warwickshire, under the patronage of the Wiggin family; of half-a-hundred villages in Northumberland—that last of the feudal counties—where a duke and many lesser lords reside *in loco parentis*.

No amount of down-grading will cause the truth to budge; and the truth is, men in deep country still look to a father-figure—not a Roman *paterfamilias* with power of life and limb, nor an Edwardian JP with power of livelihood and eviction, but a countryman who is compassionate, wise, influential. In short, the most fortunate villagers are those who, when they need advice or a contribution, can approach the manor with no more deference than courtesy requires.

In the Garden

A cottage garden suggests thatched eaves, trim lawns, and hollyhocks peering over hedges. Just such a garden lies beyond the village school. Roses really do grow round the door. The lawn is so small that the mower never has time to get under way. Year after year the same flowers appear in the same places; not because the gardener knows no others, or cannot afford to buy them, but because 'the old familiar faces' please him so well that he feels no inclination to supplant them. There is an arbour in the garden, roofed with honeysuckle, and under it a seat, on which the cottager, having laboured for six days, rests during the seventh, and finds that his handiwork is good. Often I see him among his flowers, taking a turn in the cool of the evening while bats flit through the fragrance of new-mown grass.

Within a middle-aged lifetime the craft of gardening has become a technological byproduct of science. In time, no doubt, a self-spraying weed will appear, causing the last of the hedgerows to disappear, so that sparrows, which formerly fetched four-for-a-farthing, will become costlier than grouse. Then at last the International Disaster Board will employ scientists to redress the balance of Mammon. But our gardening journalists are by no means a new species. In 1572 a silviculturist published *Arte and*

graffing and planting of trees; in 1664 came *Compleat gardiner's practice*
and *England's happiness increased . . . potatoes*. In 1710 the book trade
began to tap an unfailing market with *Young gardener's directory*;
eleven years later the manor house ordered a copy of the new
Country housewife and lady's director. At about the same time the
craze for foreign fashions was excited and appeased by *French
gardiner . . . fruit trees and herbs* and by a more literal *politesse* in
Nouveau traite pour la culture des fleurs.

All that, of course, was in prose; but some of the horticulturists
composed poems. Vergil started the thing, and it was still flourishing in 1557 when Thomas Tusser published *A hundredth good
points of husbandrie*. Two centuries later Christopher Smart produced a textbook for Augustans:

> When to inhume the plants; to turn the glebe;
> And wed the tendrils to th'aspiring poles;
> Under what sign to pluck the crop, and how
> To cure and in capacious sacks infold,
> I teach in verse Miltonian.

James Thomson remained content with a more general treatment,
The Seasons, yet he admired *Cyder*—Philips's textbook for apple-
growers—in which the poet foretold (mistakenly) that cider

> shall please all tastes, and triumph o'er the vine. . . .

Bombarded by such expertise, veteran cottagers now sit at the feet
of a young Bachelor of Bacteriology, not always meekly, for,
when the Bachelor has ended his homily, Benedict will sometimes
mutter: "Reckon my old grannie knew all that afore she was so-
high."

In an era when bombs were cheaper than they are now, and
adolescence less eager to appear prematurely aged, Robert
Bridges sat in his garden, admiring the flowers while he browsed
on Homer. So rapt was his reverie, he quite forgot the busy
world that

> Toiled, moiled, fussed, scurried,
> Worried, bought and sold,
> Plotted, stole and quarrelled,
> Fought and God knows what.

There lies the deepest dichotomy, not only between men but also
within man himself—the active versus a contemplative life; and

gardening draws the pair together. The hours spent working in a garden deserve to be included among what Wordsworth called "that best portion of a good man's life". To Francis Bacon—even although he was a bad man—a garden seemed "the purest of all pleasures". Some people will agree with Addison when he confessed: "I value my garden more for being full of blackbirds than of cherries." Fruit or flute, a gardener observes many life-cycles before his own is ended.

The creator of Sherlock Holmes set great store by the flowers:

"Our highest assurance of the goodness of Providence," wrote Dr Conan Doyle, "seems to me to rest in the flowers." Those gifts, he affirmed, are not necessary to our existence; they come as an extra delight: "It is only goodness which gives extras, and so I say again that we have much to hope from the flowers." Any sixth-former will detect the assumption in Doyle's argument; yet, by emphasising the mystery, his conclusion invites the scientific attitude to remember that doubt is not the same as dogma.

Nowadays the heirs of Capability Brown ply a brisk trade, laying-out a dozen acres, or designing a few yards of rock garden. Brown himself began as gardener to Sir William Loraine, lord of the manor of Kirkharle, that compact hamlet in Northumberland. Even today you can see traces of Brown's early talent there, in the site of an avenue and in the shadow of a mound. To most people, however, a gardener is a man who tends, and has perhaps created, his own paradise. Croesus cannot buy the gardener's achievement, for it belongs solely to those who trim their own borders, weed their own flower beds, clip their own hedges, heap their own humus. It may be said of such men that each has planted a garden of Eden (no doubt with the help of Eve), all the more real because slugs and other serpents cause a load of mischief. Nine-tenths of our gardens are in towns, and many of them testify to the zeal with which their owners serve the cause of beauty and contentment. Have you ever explored the back streets of Poplar, or Wigan, or Glasgow? If you have, you will admire the fierce fight against ugliness that is waged there, literally inch by inch across a few feet of sooty soil. Gardeners are warriors waging a beneficent warfare.

And yet, after all, the town garden is at best an oasis in a desert of cement, whereas country gardens are gardens within a garden. But whether on a hill or in a slum, all true gardeners accept a symbolic saying: "And the Lord God took the man, and put him in the garden of Eden to dress it and keep it."

Best of Both Worlds

All night the boat had swayed in the beam of the lighthouse, but toward dawn, when the breeze dropped, the morning star hovered unveering at the masthead. The sea was so calm that it made no stir, not even against the clinker hull. It hardly seemed possible that one could lie offshore with so little movement and without a sound.

At dusk on the previous evening I had steered down-stream in time to see the gay frocks and pink table lamps of diners at the quayside hotel. One mermaiden swam across the harbour, and with each stroke the sea caught fire, green fire, flecked with white. Terrace upon terrace, the cliffside houses shone like tinted glow-worms. Regular as clockwork, the lighthouse flashed a fairway through dark waters, and was answered by the Lizard light sweeping a westward sky.

Having passed the lighthouse, I came about, and dropped anchor in the sand. Then I went below for supper. Afterwards I lit a pipe, returned on deck, checked anchor and riding light, and leaned against the wheel. Inland a sheep bleated just loud enough

to reach me on a breeze; seaward a tanker mimed a moving hotel; above, the Pole Star held its course. Traherne understood: "You will never enjoy the world aright, till the sea itself floweth in your veins, till you are clothed with the heavens, and crowned with the stars."

Noah's Ark carried two passengers, a young couple fond of fishing for bass from a dinghy. This voyage through deeper waters was an invitation which they had accepted gladly. So, between dozing and watchkeeping, I left them to it until, as I say, the sun rose, and the wind dropped. The deck meanwhile resembled a fishmonger's slab whereon we ate the new-caught bass, each gourmet clasping the roof of a buttered cottage loaf, and a mug of sugarful cocoa. Then we upped anchor, and returned to harbour, *Noah's Ark* swishing and surging and altogether singing a shanty to the sea. We tied up, brewed some more cocoa, and then went shopping. So lately at sea, we were landsmen again, having enjoyed the best of both worlds, among a breed from whom Joseph Conrad learned his own seamanship. "Coast men," he called them, "with steady eyes, mighty limbs, gentle voices; men of very few words. . . . Honest, strong, steady men, sobered by domestic ties." Those men are still alive. You will find them in Yorkshire, up an Essex creek, on the Welsh coast, in Scottish waters. I know of one Devonian whose boat is moored alongside his tractor. While the sun shines he tills his fields, and when it sets you will see him at the tiller, oilskinned and spume-sprayed, reaping a harvest from the sea. Insofar as he sails some-times to Spain, he is an heir of Chaucer's shipman:

> He knew well all the havens, as they were,
> From Gootland to the Cape of Finisterre,
> And every creek in Brittany and Spain.

No other discipline excels the sea's ability to brace the body, to sharpen the wits, to refresh the imagination. Moreover the sea speaks its own language: port, starboard, knittles, casco, bit-terend, lee cro'jack, vulgar establishment, Dutchman's log . . . all those words say what they mean, and no other words say it so well. The smaller the ship, the greater her capacity to practice a skill that has been outmoded by machines. Shakespeare made his seamen jump to it in *The Tempest*: "speak to the mariners; fall to it, yarely, or we run ourselves aground. Bestir, bestir." Like Gon-zalo, many a landsman has found courage in the boatswain's rough demeanour: "I take great comfort from this fellow, me-thinks he hath no drowning mark upon him; his complexion is perfect gallows."

It is a fact of history that no nation was so famous as the English for their seamanship in war and peace. England not only ruled the waves but also co-opted them as part of herself: "If you are born in any ship, provided she is under sail, you are English-born. By virtue of the age-old customs of London, the waves are part of England." That is not an Englishman's boast; it was an international *fait accompli*, recorded in the *Memoirs* of François-René de Chateaubriand, Foreign Minister to King Louis XVIII. To live in a small boat, with the sea as a highway, and saltwater creeks as byeways, is to make both landfalls and seafalls; savouring solitude without losing fellowship. Anchored in mid-stream, you feel more secluded than on Ben Nevis; coming alongside the jetty, you feel more gregarious than in Piccadilly. On Monday you are literally all at sea; on Tuesday, mowing a friend's meadow; on Wednesday, catching bass by moonlight. Unlike the oceanic mariner or a shire grazier, you may come and go as you please, sailing out to sea or up to Truro.

"The sea," declared Euripedes, "washes away the ills of men." And the sea is itself wherever it flows, whether in mid-Atlantic or westward of Fowey. More than one mariner in trouble off the Manacles has remembered his Prayer Book: "Look down we beseech thee, and hear us, calling out of the depth of misery, and out of the jaws of this death, which is ready now to swallow us up." At such moments not even a philosopher questions the ordering of events. Finding himself alive and still afloat, he utters the thanks of Nelson's seamen: "Thou didst send forth thy commandment; and the windy storm ceased, and was turned into a calm."

And there is another saying: "They that go down to the sea in ships: and occupy their business in great waters; these men see the works of the Lord; and his wonders in the deep." Still from the cockpit of a yacht, or on the bridge of a steamer, the 'coast men' watch those old words come true; they whose little ships wrote *Dunkirk* indelibly in sand and water; they whose legs are as steady on a rolling deck as down a winding lane; they who follow the light that always was on sea and land. But a price must be paid for enjoying the best of both worlds, and sometimes it will seem heavy, for when the gulls glide inland, scavenging the fields, every man who has loved his ship confronts a famous conflict:

I must go down to the seas again, to the lonely sea
and the sky,
And all I ask is a tall ship and a star to steer
her by.

Scorched Earth

The drought was becoming serious. Cracks had appeared in the clay, and all meadows were stunted. Hollyhocks drooped, sagging from their stakes. Water-troughs in far fields were tepid. Ruts on a cart-track seemed to have been grooved in cement. The upland streams were so fissured that you could thrust three fingers into the bed. One spark might have kindled two fields. The land was as scorched as James Thomson's:

> Deep to the root
> Of vegetation parched, the cleaving fields
> And slippery lawn an arid hue disclose

The stockman expressed it more emphatically: "Whole bloody place stinks." And he was right because decaying matter had lain for weeks in every ditch and brook. Shakespeare merged optimistic with pessimism when he complained "the rain it raineth every day".

Then at last came the cloud that was no bigger than a man's hand. I watched it arrive, a white sail on a blue sea. Again the stockman spoke: "I'd almost forgotten what one o' them bloody things looked like." The man himself, by the way, was in every sense a sanguinary person, to whom 'bloody' meant no more than an emphatic grunt. They used to say that whenever he cut himself while shaving he would mutter: "This bloody blood."

Meanwhile we both gazed up as the lone cloud drew nearer and was followed by others. Within an hour the air had become so heavy that it lay on our chests without helping us to breathe. At teatime the world went as dark as Thomson's falling barometer:

> Thick clouds ascend, in whose capacious womb
> A vapoury deluge lies. . . .

During the lull I pondered the role of water on this earth. A human being, for example, creates almost a pint of it in the daily oxidising of his food, but loses five pints through other bodily processes. Few men can live above ten days without liquid. Plants are more resourceful because they delve deeply when the moisture level sinks. Rain, however, is more than a thirst-quencher, for it dissolves certain gases in the air, notably oxygen and nitrogen with traces of ammonia and carbonic acid. Nitrogen, in fact, is rain's most valuable contribution to the soil, and farmers buy it expensively as an artificial fertiliser. Between 1865 and 1880 an analysis was made of rain water in various parts of Europe, the average annual yield of nitrogen per acre being 10·23 pounds. At Rothamstead in Hertfordshire the annual yield was about five pounds per acre, conspicuously below average.

Even after Tennyson's "burning drouth" the soil and its creatures may recover quickly. I remembered driving through Cumberland during a dry spell when the cattle looked as lean as the land. That night it rained and far into the next day. On the fourth morning, happening to pass the same herd, I was so struck by their improved appearance that I stopped to ask the farmer whether I had imagined it. He shook his head: "Nay, thou's not imagining. Look at yon grass in't slack. Three days ago it were a sand pit. Now 'tis summat for 'em to graze."

Then the lull ended, and my Cumbrian recollections were shattered by a crackle of thunder. The first drop fell like a dimple on the waterbutt. The second arrived with such eagerness that it plopped up again. Soon the roof of a Dutch barn rattled to the sound of liquid pellets; within thirty seconds the scorched earth was hissing. After weeks of sunshine we were content—we were thankful—to greet dark skies, swirling mist, sodden meadows. In normal times a heavy downpour causes the moorland streams to rise visibly within minutes, but after prolonged drought the earth will swallow vast quantities of water without as it were dribbling one drop.

To watch the rain when it is overdue can seem as refreshing as to feel the sun when that too has lagged behind. Not troubling to fetch a macintosh, I stood in the farmer's garden while the beige flowerbeds deepened to a plum pudden tilth. I watched those wilting hollyhocks that now winced with every gust as though they had mixed their metaphors by supposing that the first drops were the last straw. In a few hours they would take new strength upward along tall spines and downward through gaping stomata. I watched the lawn while it changed from pale brown to dark; and that, too, would coax old colour from new comfort. The birds waited beside empty puddle-holes, like men when they have turned on the bath tap. Then I glanced at a holly bush, and saw that its topmost leaves had already shed the dust which still clung to lower boughs. In the shippon a cargo of chaff and straw went surging through conduits. Blocked gutters brimmed over and then fell down, sheer as a mountain beck. Friesians grazing the fields resembled skew-bald sou'esters in a gale. Only the cat seemed displeased, and had retreated to the porch, where she licked her matted haunches. Everyone else and everywhere else looked better and felt better. It was as though a celestial window had been opened, admitting not only the rain but also a breeze that swept away all cobwebs, and in their place set the soil's natural fragrance, down to earth because up from earth, an attic of green grass and fresh air.

Peering through a stable door, the farmer surveyed the change of scene with such complacency that he hardly noticed the deluge which had extinguished his pipe. Five matches he struck, and still the tobacco remained highly non-inflammable. Then from his poacher's pocket he produced a lighter whose flame could have set the Thames on fire, or melted bars at the Bank of England. The aftermath was not fragrant, yet the farmer held it close to his nostrils, rather as though, like everything else, it had been sweetened by the rain. As for the stockman, he was moved beyond his customary word. All he said was: "And about time, too."

In September, when the autumn rains arrive, we shall greet them with a tinge of melancholy, for they come to summon summer. But in June the season is young, and when the rain has refreshed it, we turn again to   ·

thinking on fantastic summer's heat.

7

Lux Mundi

Everyone feels better when the sun shines. Blinking through the gloom of his backroom workshop, the village carpenter looks up with a smile: "Lovely day again." And how often has a greybeard defied his rheumatism by exclaiming: "Treat to be alive." William Blake extended an invitation both immanent and transcendent:

> Look at the rising sun: there God does live,
> And gives His light, and gives His heat away;
> And flowers and trees and beasts and men receive
> Comfort in morning, joy in the noonday.

Our search for the sun is simplified by atlases which tell us where to find it. The south coast wins first place, for Ventnor enjoys nearly 1,800 hours of annual sunshine, and Eastbourne basks even more benignly. On that point, however, patriotism tends to become another name for profit, with East Anglian chambers of commerce retorting that Felixstowe gives nearly as much sunshine as Penzance, and a lot less rain. I fancy, though, that Manchester Corporation will not take up those climatic cudgels, for their city offers less than 970 hours of sunlight. Manchester, in fact, lies at the very bottom of the lowest division in the sunshine league. Even Aberdeen, that frigid place, is 50 per cent brighter in summer. But the statistics must be interpreted carefully. Borrowdale, for example, is the wettest place in England, yet its yearly sunshine exceeds Burnley's in Lancashire. Britain's least sunny spots are among the central northern Highlands of Scotland and thence up to Caithness, except near the coast, where Wick enjoys more than 1,400 hours of sun (and how gaily the many-coloured fishing vessels reflect that boon). London more or less ties with Wick, having about 1,460 hours each year.

Nowadays we regard the sun chiefly as an ally of our playful occasions. Yet even at Boscombe the grilled sardines experience something of the exultant awe with which their distant forebears served the great god, Shakespeare's "worshipped sun". Our Yule log is but a christened convert, a relic of those wintry fires which cavemen lit to revive a dying sun; so also are the Christmas evergreens whose immortality was supposed to work sympathetic magic at a time of death and dearth. Poets have indeed warmed the world with their songs to the light of the world, *Lux mundi*. Burns bade us "adore the morning sun". Masefield chose sunlight as the soul's balm: "The morning comes with all-refreshing dew." Leconte de Lisle saluted it as regal: *Midi, roi des étés*; Sir Thomas Wyatt admired it as "all-glorious"; Campion, as "heavenly"; Burns, as "braw" or brave; Laurence Binyon, as "miraculous"; Maurice Hewlett, as "the comforter". Even Thomas Hardy looked up from his tombstones to remark:

> This is the weather the cuckoo likes,
> And so do I. . . .

In the evening—"the light of setting suns"—Wordsworth saw what St Augustine called "our rest in Thee". Vaughan, too, equated light with life: "They are all gone into the world of light." Poets and ploughmen alike understand the sibilant saying, *Sine sole sileo*, "Without the sun I am silent."

Commonsense finds nothing excessive in those avowals. All men are creatures, which is to say unself-created, and some of them have not yet aped the new gods, the machines, which cannot enjoy the light that sets a smile upon the face of the earth, making dark things bright, and brightness brilliant. Who has not stood on a hill in summer, watching the cloud-shadows move like sombre fingers steeped in pale green paint? Who has not blinked to behold the grey sea transmuted into a blue cauldron minting its golden guineas? Who has not emerged from an alley into the warmth "on the sunny side of the street"? Does not every man assume his right to "a place in the sun"? A fortunate few need not wait precariously on a high summer fortnight; like Chaucer they make merry betimes:

> When that the month of May
> Is comen and I hear the fowlys sing,
> Farewell my book and my devocioun!

Farmfolk and fishermen stay breeze-brown throughout the year, but in July their tan ripens to a Majorcan mahogany. The men themselves set no great store by it; like the miller's pallor, it is a trademark and no more. By way of parasol they wear a cap. Some wear it all day and every day; nor do they consider it discourteous to wear the cap indoors. As a result, many farmers appear skew-bald when at last they do uncover, being brick-brown below the eye brows, and milk-white above. In my young days I used to visit a sheep farm whose hands supped in the kitchen at shearing time. On first entering the room I took off my cap, whereupon each man removed his own . . . and then replaced it. On the third evening—the same brief courtesies having been observed—a veteran rebuked me gently: "Nay, lad, don't thee fidget so." Thereafter, as the Royal Navy says, I maintained the rule of On Caps. But agriculture has no monopoly of sunshine. Pen-pushing, too, may lose its pallor in July. When Galsworthy was living in Devonshire he had a semi-circle of desks and chairs on the lawn, so arranged that, like the shadow on a sundial, he and his papers could move with the times.

Meanwhile, the whole kingdom praises the sun, as though Albion were Milton's paradise:

> There eternal summer dwells. . . .

Down in Cornwall the weather forecast says: "Us be going to sizzle come dinner time." Up in Scotland—where temperament and temperature are less lyrical—the dominie remarks: "I'm thinking I'll no' need a jacket." And in Wales a housewife tempers her praise with a plaint: "Evans Milk, can't you leave the bottle in the shade, man?"

Everywhere it is the same. Whenever the sun shines, his subjects prove their fealty. Old dogs lie in the middle of lanes, content to know that their season of new tricks has given way to a more restful expertise. Outside the pub, beer-mugged men warm their backsides on a sun-drenched seat. Ploughboys go courting. Shepherds walk whistling. Life is worth living.

A Day of Unrest

Sunday never was so good as it used to be, nor ever so bad except to those who, knowing nothing better than the present, assume that everything past must have been worse. When summer calls out the cars, not a few villagers look back to Abelard's more restful era:

> O quanta qualia
> Sunt illa Sabbata!

Sunday, the first day of a Christian week, is not Sabbath, the last day of a Jewish week. The Rabbis devised a Sabbath-day's journey of 1,125 yards, which, they decided, was as far as a man might travel on that day. According to Jeremy Taylor "The Primitive Church kept both the Sabbath and the Lord's Day." Our own Sunday is the Greek *heemera heeliou* or day of the sun, adopted to commemorate the Resurrection. Torn between Christianity and Judaism, the Bible has confounded us. Keats and Shelley wrote 'Sabbath' when they ought to have written 'Sunday'. Alexander Pope equated the days algebraically by complaining "Sunday shines no Sabbath-day for me".

One fact, however, is beyond dispute: Sunday used to be a day of rest. Men had worked hard for six days, and on the seventh they followed the example of their Maker, who, they believed, chose the Sabbath as a season of voluntary absenteeism. On that day the villagers of my childhood advanced their breakfast-time from seven to nine o'clock; and although they did not lie abed until the beer or the BBC had made consciousness bearable, it was unusual to meet them in the street before ten, at which hour the pageant of church and chapel got under way. Some of the dissenters obeyed both the letter and the spirit of what they regarded as God's law, but most of the Anglicans saw nothing amiss in a glass of ale after the sermon. On Sunday afternoon even the busiest housewife wore a best bonnet and strolled with her man in the sun. That pleasant custom is dying from the countryside; and so also is the button-hole which went with it, fresh-cut from the garden or from a flower-bed on the allotment.

Of the lovers and other young people long ago I cannot speak with authority, because my own libido was at that time directed toward toffee and trains. I would suggest, though, that it was easier then than now to sift the male from the female of the species, and that their clothes were sometimes more comely and often more cumbersome than ours. Of the differences between righteousness then and now I shall say nothing, except to remark that places of worship which were half-full are now two-thirds empty. There was a fair amount of fornication in those days and a similar quantity of hypocrisy; but only to a very small elect had God revealed that he did not exist.

Under whatever name, Sunday was baptised by the fourth commandment: "Remember that thou keep holy the Sabbath day. . . . In it thou shalt do no manner of work, thou, and thy son, and thy daughter, thy man-servant and thy maid-servant, thy cattle, and the stranger that is within thy gates." Scions of compulsory education and the scientific attitude may ask to know the reason for that uneconomic anachronism; to whom the Bible replies: "in six days the Lord made heaven and earth, the sea, and all that in them is, and rested the seventh day: wherefore the Lord blessed the seventh day, and hallowed it." Few of us feel obliged to accept a literal translation of the second book of Moses. No doubt the forward-looking Bishop of Eatanswill would wish to abolish Sunday because of its associations with Hildebrand, Luther, and other bourgeois Fundamentalists. But why bother to destroy what the majority of Britons have already discarded? Even the therapeutic arguments in favour of relaxation will seem outdated when technology condemns us to six days of leisure.

Looking back on his American home, Nathaniel Hawthorne harboured what he called "Severe and sunless recollections of the Sabbaths of childhood." Truly the Pilgrims were not always wise Fathers. Children, perhaps, did receive a raw deal on Sunday; yet they were not utterly downcast. Instead of stirring their latency by watching Sex For Six Year Olds, they responded to the story of Daniel in the den, or David and Goliath, or Ruth amid the alien corn. True, there was an air of self-denial on Sunday, especially among the dissenters and evangelicals; but it cannot have been entirely harmful for children to acquire a firm conviction that unselfishness exists and may prove salutary to all whom it concerns.

Now at last those faraway days are called 'dead'. But they were not dead. They were sleeping or relaxing themselves. Above all, they differed from the other six days. No such charge can be laid against the modern fashion, which, in the words of *Hamlet*, "does not divide the Sunday from the rest of the week". Our hospitals overflow with impatients who have hurried themselves into emotional illness. Only the most urgent private summons will persuade me to make a long summer journey between noon on Friday and midnight on Sunday. Thoreau himself ridiculed those busybodies who rush from place to place in search of nothing worth finding: "It is not worth while," he said, "to go round the world to count the cats in Zanzibar." Yet the counting continues and has become obsessive. Instead of waking to the leisurely quietness with which the village used to spend Sunday, people are alarmed at 9 a.m. when the one-man garage opens fire with three motor-cycles. Although I live too far from any village to be disturbed by its contemporary forms of worship, I have observed that at ten o'clock a posse of beetle-black Martians emerge from their mechanised stables. By midday a crescendo of cars has beseiged the pub. Throughout the afternoon a noxious crocodile threshes the roads of Britain.

> It was a summer's evening,
> Old Kaspar's work was done,
> And he before his cottage door
> Was sitting in the sun.

Not nowadays he isn't. He sits in his car—and the rest of a grizzling family with him—traffic-jammed eastward of Exeter or six miles short of Windermere. A brief lull follows until at sundown the motoring hordes return home, wondering why they will feel weary on Monday morning.

The era of leisure has murdered repose.

Country Talk

The windows of the school were open to admit the sun. Through them I overheard the master discussing holidays. Being a Westmorlander he spoke of the 'skule', the school. His was true country talk, born centuries ago, modified by time, and still going strong despite evil communications.

Westmorland, of course, is a small county and sparsely popu-
lated; yet the Kirkby Lonsdale accent differs from Kendal's,
scarcely a dozen miles away. You find a comparable variety among
the Chiltern Hills, where the villagers of Dunsmore in Buckinghamshire speak with an accent that differs from Ipsden's in
Oxfordshire. Subtler still is the change that travels northward
from Alston in Cumberland to Slaggyford in Northumberland, a
journey of less than five miles. Indeed, the nuances of country
talk are sometimes so subtle that they cannot be translated
phonetically. William Barnes tried to speak for Dorset:

> An' brown-leaf'd fruits a-turnen red
> In cloudless zunsheen, auver head,
> Wi' fruit vor me, the apple tree
> Do lean down low in Linden lea.

Tennyson tried to catch the timbre of his Lincolnshire Wolds:

> Parson's lass 'ant nowt, an' she weant 'a nowt
> when 'e's dead;
> Mun be a governess, lad, or summut, and addle her
> bread. . . .

But the eye soon wearies of its effort to feed the ear. The printed
word remains dumb unless a reader has the melody by heart.
Artistry may suggest, but it can never become a tape-recorder.

The best-known dialect—Lancashire's—achieved a theatrical
fame via Gracie Fields. Few southrons, however, could dis-
tinguish between the talk of a Chorley tradesman and a Yorkshire
shepherd from Hawes. The West Country, too, suffers a theatrical
confusion, chiefly because of the spurious Zummerzet patois
which London audiences accept as the very voice of England
westward from Bournemouth. In fact, that voice can be detected
so far to the east as Burford in Oxfordshire; and a few miles
beyond Burford, at Lechlade in Wiltshire, the voice becomes un-
mistakable.

Why, one asks, was this small island set to so many sorts of
music? The answer lies in the islanders' hybrid ancestry, for our
country talk is a dilution not of a single norm, but of the several
languages that were spoken by Celts, Jutes, Angles, Saxons,
Normans; all leavened with Latin, tinctured with Greek, vulgar-
ised by America, contorted by technology. Five hundred years
ago a Tynesider would not have been able to understand a

Cornishman, and each would have sounded unintelligible to a Kentish man. William Caxton, our pioneer printer, tells of a traveller who, having asked his hostess for eggs or *egges*, was affronted when the woman replied that she could not speak French: in her part of England *egges* were *eyren*. Something of that diversity survives today, because dialect is not solely a matter of accent; the words and their syntax vary from county to county. An elderly Chiltern cottager will complain that his neighbour is *pimmocky* or over-fastidious; a Cumbrian will remark that a shower of rain has made the world seem *grosky* or green; in Cambridgeshire they speak of *frumenty* or wheat boiled in spice; in Cornwall a 'zany' means a simpleton; in Yorkshire a finicky person is *kysty*; in Westmorland a farmhand is a *hind*; in Derbyshire you still hear *wacken* or wideawake; in Shropshire a hill is a 'bank'.

Unlike the Germans and the French, most Britons long ago discarded the intimacy of 'thou' and 'thee', preferring to address their beloved as though she were a public meeting (the 1640 edition of Jonson's *Grammar* contained the word 'yee'; but in 1692 the entry became 'you'). In the north of England, however, the farmfolk maintain the ancient courtesies: "Thee mun gang along" means, in southern slang, "Get cracking." Echoes of a Teutonic *er ist* still resound, when instead of asking, "How are you?" a Lakelander says ,"Ist still alive?"

Some tones of talk sound downright ugly to ears that have no affinity with the region. Few strangers find euphony in the dialect of Bedfordshire or of Essex, which resemble Cockney. Generally we prefer the dialects that are most familiar to us. Beatrix Potter confessed: "To me no tongue can be as musical as Lancashire" (but the sturdy sheep-farmer dwelt among the Lancashire mountains, which echo the melodies of Westmorland and Cumberland). Most people are surprised when they learn that more than half a dozen languages are spoken by natives of the United Kingdom: English, Welsh, Gaelic, several varieties of Channel Island French, and—on State occasions—Manx in the Isle of Man. Down in Cornwall they are trying to revive their own ancient tongue, but the attempt was stillborn because Cornish will never again be a living language, spoken daily across the counter, as are Gaelic and Welsh. Moreover, Cornish has scarcely any extant literature.

The most vivid contrasts occur in border country. Near Kirk Yetholm I have met roadmen speaking deepest Northumbrian; and after three hundred yards, having entered Roxburghshire, I heard the braw lads in their Lowland Scots, that is, their Highland English, the dialect having crossed the Cheviots from Northumberland. Roman gourmets claimed that their palate could decide from what stretch of the Tiber a fish had been taken. British auditors claim that their ear can decide upon what side of the Tamar a man had been born. What, you may ask, is the point of country talk? The best answer is another question: "What is the point of twilight, or of rose-scent, or of a gull's wings when they catch the sun?" Country talk recalls and helps to perpetuate the fact that, more than any other land of similar size, England is less a nation than a concomitance of counties. Fifty years ago the cottagers spoke with an accent that baffled people who had not been bred upon it. The great-grandchildren of those cottagers still do speak rustically, but their tone of voice is being changed by whatever jargon they overhear via London. Tuppence-coloured sounds to some ears more pleasing than penny-plain; to others it is an anachronism, an echo from distinctive classes, soon to be drowned by the high winds of change; but not too soon, for if a Yorkshire child were to catch someone trying to steal the farmer's hurricane lamp, he would still utter the hue-and-cry of Joseph in *Wuthering Heights*: "Maister, maister, he's stealing t'lanthern!"

The Lane to Arcady

There is one tone of country talk that seems unlikely to change within the foreseeable future. It can be heard every day and many times a day from Land's End to Loweswater, from the Severn at Shrewsbury to the sea at Sheringham. I mean, of course, our English place-names.

Up in Durham I had cause to ask the way to Pity Me, a name likely to perplex even the plurimi-linguist. Various romantic etymologies came to mind. Was there a castle at Pity Me, and in it the ghost of a captive heiress? Did a martyr die there? Or was the place baptised by a Provençal knight as he gazed at a dour land, dreaming of his native sunshine? France had certainly christened the spot, but never for pity's sake; the name is a corruption of *petit mer*, the French monks' translation of a small lake nearby. In the East Riding of Yorkshire you will find a place called Haltemprice; and that, too, sounds meaningless until you discover that in 1322 a party of Frenchman, having founded a monastery there, with pious pride described the foundation as a high enterprise or *haut emprise*, which Oakroyd and his kin have anglicised as Haltemprice.

Walkers who follow the Icknield Way through Oxfordshire may remember the village of Britwell Salome, whose second name recalls Herod's decapitating dancer. But the lady herself never passed that way, nor did the villagers co-opt her as a distinguished synonym. In 1322 Britwell Salome was *Brutewelle Solham* or the place beside a bright stream, belonging to the Suleham family. In 1236 the manor had been held by Aumaricus de Suleham, who migrated thither from Sulham in Berkshire (Sulham being a variant of the Old English *sulh* or narrow valley).

At this point a potential place-namer may well give up the game, fearing that it has no rules. Such despair is ill-founded. True, an etymologist must have Old English, Old Welsh, Old French, Old Norse, with some Latin, some Greek, and a smatter of Arabic, Cornish, and several Indian dialects: true also that *in extremis* he may wish that he had realised T. S. Eliot's ideal of a literary man's repertoire: "Hebrew suggests itself, but both for extreme difference of structure and intellectual dignity a very good choice would be Chinese. . . ." There are occasions when not even a knowledge of Chinese can translate a place-name into modern English. I think of the North Devon signpost (parenthetically Unfit For Motor Vehicles) which points to Kemacott and Kittitoe. A philologist might trace the ancestry of those names, but only the native knows that each is a private house and that one had been a farm. Even so, a monoglot traveller in Britain still has some signposts to guide him, erected by Celt, Roman, Saxon, Viking, Norman. Thus, the Roman *castra* or camp became the Old English *ceaster*, and is to be found at Manchester, Lancaster, Alcester. The Saxon *tun* or township is common, as at Luton, Tunstall, Northampton. Thorpe, on the other hand, came from Denmark, where it meant a hamlet; in England you may use it to trace the Viking incursions overland via creeks. Another Scandinavian word, *by*, means a homestead or a village; and that, too, is common, as at Busby and Harrowby. The word *leah*—meaning a clearing in a wood, and sometimes a low-lying meadow—appears variously as ley, leigh, leam. Obvious examples are Wheatley, Stockleigh, Leamington. The retreating Celts can be traced via *trev* and *tre*, the old Cornish words for a homestead: Tregair, Tregarn, Tremaine.

Philology is usually able to solve its own problems, as at Upper and Lower Slaughter, two peaceful places, whose names, though they suggest scenes of Cotswold carnage, recall rather that

the villages were built on land which the Saxons named a *sloghtre* or slough. In some places, however, philology falls short of its destination. The traveller must then become a blend of historian and folklorist. Consider, for instance, the Somerset village of Queen Camel, which was presented to Queen Eleanor by Edward I in or about the year 1280. The regal prefix explains itself; but whence came the camels and why? Not even the zaniest west-countryman will suppose that camels were once indigenous to the district; and since Queen Camel lies a longish way from the alleged site of Camelot, it can scarcely be interpreted as an abbreviation of King Arthur's Court. But softly: is there not a River Camel in Somerset? Clearly, then, the village was baptised in its water; an ingenious guess but also a wide miss, for Camel is the name of a local hill which itself echoes an Old Welsh word, *cant*, meaning a rim or skyline.

In these matters caution must be the password, and history the reply. Thus, the name of Marazion, a hamlet of Penzance, was formerly *Marghasbighan*, from two Cornish words, *marchas* or market and *bichan* or small. One would assume, therefore, that Marazion had received its charter from the King or some other magnate. But not so; the right to hold a Thursday market was granted to the monastery on St Michael's Mount, facing Marazion from the sea; and because time and tide are entirely without business experience, the monks held their market on the mainland.

All this may have left the wayfarer bewildered by his own ignorance of mediaeval law and Dark Age Danish. Yet in that darkness a light shineth, a constellation of practical poetry composed by our forefathers. And what compositions! They trip from the tongue. They are a secular window of Jesse, telling not only where we would go but also whence we have come. Listen to their music: Predannack Warras, Amalabrea, Chyandor, Maidens Grove, Christmas Common, Velvet Lawn, High Heaven, Sco Rushton, Bix, Mavis Enderby, Edith Weston, Langton-juxta-Partney, Indio, Idle, Barton-in-the-Beans, St Anthony-in-Roseland, Hensington-Within-and-Without, Guiting Power, Come-to-Good, Ding-Dong, Indian Queens, Paradise, Hell, Egypt, Gibraltar, Drunken Bottom, God's Garden. A poet once set those facts to music:

> The fingerposts of England
> Make native melodies,
> Descanting on the courses
> To hidden Arcadies.

Travellers in High Places

The word 'mountain' evokes an exalted image. Among people who live far from high places the image may be vague and romantic, a blend of Landseer and Switzerland. Among people who do live in high places the image becomes more precise. Yet the mountains themselves will often change their appearance. There is snow-streaked Helvellyn, seen from the shale slopes above Wythburn; there is sunlit Helvellyn, smiling on Patterdale; and there is invisible Helvellyn, with only its toes piercing a mist. But whether visible or invisible, all mountains utter a challenge, for their voice is the wind's voice, pitched higher than the cloud which it impales. High therefore is the mood—though deep the speech—of men who possess not only the stamina to reach those heights but also the eloquence that evokes them. Hilaire Belloc, palmering the road to Rome, was stopped in his tracks: "Sky beneath them and sky above them, a steadfast legion, they glittered as though with the armour of the immovable armies of Heaven. Two days' march, three days' march away . . . here were the magnificent creatures of God, I mean the Alps, which now for the first time I saw from the heights of Jura. . . ."

Amid that exalted company it may sound prosaic to ask what a mountain is. The Himalayans, no doubt, regard it as anything higher than Mont Blanc; among Fensmen it is anything above their own chimney pots. In England and Wales, they say, a mountain must be at least two thousand feet high. There are six hundred and twelve such summits. Scotland is more ambitious. There a mountain must reach three thousand feet, which was the height chosen by Sir Hugh Munro for his list of Scottish peaks. Having scaled all but two of them, he discovered five hundred and thirty-eight summits above three thousand feet. The rest of the kingdom lags far below Scotland's total. Wales has only sixteen summits above three thousand feet; Northern Ireland has eleven; England has seven (and all of them are in the North Country).

High places bear several generic names. England has Dunkery Beacon, Rough Tor, Coombe Hill, Scafell Pike, Penistone Crag, Shap Fell; Scotland has Braigh, Squrr, Beinn, Mam, Noel, Creag, Druim, Bidean, Meall, Monadh, Sron, Srac, Scob; Wales has Myndd, Bryn, Carreg, Moel, Rhos. The least familiar style is Forest, which in Scotland may denote a peak higher than Snowdon. Sometimes the hills lack a courtesy title, like Brown Willy in Cornwall, and Cumberland's Blencathra or Saddleback. Sometimes, too, a mountain is called a hill, and vice-versa. Thus, having toiled nearly three thousand feet above Northumberland, you reach the summit of Cairn Hill; yet a mere five hundred feet will bring you to the top of Parys Mountain in Anglesey. Some Welshmen affect not to know that Snowdon is considerably lower than Britain's highest mountain, Ben Nevis, 4,406 feet. Some Scotsmen underrate Plynlimon, like the Braemar shepherd who said to me: "Wales? Aye, I've taken a wee stroll up the hills." Plynlimon, by the way, is Britain's most-spelt mountain, by which I mean that no other is spelt so variously. The Ordnance Survey would have us write Plumlummon. At Llanidloes, however, they spell the word according to the day of the week. As George Borrow pointed out, Plynlimon means "five points or peaks".

Some observers suppose that contact with reality is in inverse proportion to the realist's height above the sea. The lower, they say, the more real. That is true indeed of several aspects of contemporary art, but it never was true of reality. Like the cost of living, the eternal verities are as real among the mountains as they are in Mayfair, and more intensely experienced because less stifled by the swaddling clothes of sophistication. No matter how high you build your house, death and disease and disaster will overtake you. Even in the Andes they yawn, and get toothache, and fail to back the winner.

The highest summits are not always the most impressive. When Celia Fiennes first saw the Malvern Hills she cried: "The English Alps!" Certainly the Malverns carve a dramatic skyline—most dramatic, perhaps, when seen from the lane between Broadway and Chipping Campden—yet they do so despite a relatively short stature, because their highest point, the Worcestershire Beacon, 1,395 feet, is less than half as tall as Cross Fell in Cumberland.

The British cult of mountain-worship is comparatively modern, at any rate in its secular guise. Celia Fiennes dismissed the Pennine Range as "a dismal high precipice". Her opinion of the Lakeland mountains was not ecstatic: "these formidable heights". A century later, Daniel Defoe fled from Hampstead Heath, declaring that it was not "a proper situation for any but a race of mountaineers, whose lungs had been used to a rarify'd air". The Augustans' fear of mountains became so morbid that it distorted their sense perception. Venturing as far north as Crooklands, a relatively flat region near Kendal, one eighteenth-century diarist noticed a slope of about five hundred feet—"the highest hill in Westmorland" he called it—and very probably hurried south as fast as he could. Lancelot Brown won an international reputation because he was capable of softening earth's warts and protuberances into Gray's fashionable preference for "o'er-arching Groves" and "level lawn". The Ancients took a loftier view of things. Parnassus, eight thousand feet above the Aegean, was a haven of the Muses, a Poets' Corner, a Royal Academy of the artistic Establishment. Olympus—collective name of several ranges—is topped by Mount Elymbo, nearly ten thousand feet above Macedonia, where dwelt the gods and over them Zeus himself, pinnacled in a palace, *altissimus inter pares.*

By the beginning of the nineteenth century the Augustan tide had turned, and was flowing uphill. In 1798 the *European Magazine* reported: "The Lakers are those persons who visit the beautiful scenes in Cumberland and Westmorland. . . ." Wordsworth himself climbed Helvellyn when he was past seventy years old. And how beautifully his sister Dorothy described their cottage at Grasmere: "It calls home the heart to quietness." I think of that whenever I climb the steep lane which greets my own return from less exalted regions. Happy indeed is the man who lifts his eyes homeward unto the hills.

The Incompleat Angler

Day and night the stream hurries to the sea, plied by a netful of trout. And everyone except myself seems able to catch them. Never a season passes without somebody stands himself a beer while the innkeeper foretells further success by speaking of the ones which, since they did get away, must have returned to fight another fly. Izaak Walton was right when he said that fishing is a matter of predestination. Many choose, but not all are chosen; and I am beginning to think that I never shall be numbered among the elect.

The stream itself defies any textbook I ever came across. All those drawings of fly fishermen . . . the dotted lines of their impeccable arcs . . . the nonchalant wrist and cavalry elbow . . . every one is a snare or at any rate the delusion of Piscators who never saw the conspiracy of trees that stand guard over our fishes. I refer, of course, to those parts of the stream whose pools

I

are the most likely to contain fishes (everywhere else the banks
are as treeless as the Sahara). Partly, no doubt, it is a matter of
Time; not of Time to come, but of Time that went and will not
return because the locusts have digested the decades which sepa-
rate my first string-and-bread line from these belated efforts with
more sophisticated (but not more successful) equipment.

And yet I see that my complaint is less than honest. Viscount
Grey long ago revealed the reason why I and my kind must
always angle incompleatly: "As the angler looks back he thinks

less of individual captures and days than of the scenes in which he
fished." If you have studied his admirable treatise on fishing, you
may reply that Viscount Grey referred to scenes which may be
supposed to bring good luck by exacting keen observation . . . of
insects, of wind, of light and warmth and gravel. But I and my
kind are undone by our keen observation of scenes that prove
downright hostile to good luck. For example, having by chance
cast without entangling the line in a tree, I notice a blackbird six
yards away. It is no excuse to protest that Walton himself praised

the birds which "in their fixed Months warble such ditties as no art or instrument can reach to". No excuse at all: by the time the song is ended, my line has wrapped itself around a branch ten yards down-stream. Or maybe the staghounds speak, faint and far from a heather-honey hill. Then—though I pity the quarry, and upbraid the hunters—I pause to share another of Walton's *obiter dicta*: "What musick doth a pack of Dogs make to any man, whose heart and ears are so happy as to be set to the tune of such instruments." This time the rod is not even at the ready, but has slumped, as though it were the starting-flag for a tortoise race. While recouping my loses, I catch sight of a limousine crawling like a beetle up the hill a mile away. Knowing its owner to be a non-residential property-developer, I hear once more the voice of Izaak Walton: "Let me tell you, Sir, there be many men that are taken to be grave, because Nature hath made them of sowre complexion, money-getting men. . . ." Having again cast, and once more caught nothing, I am by the same voice admonished: "O Sir, doubt not but that Angling is an Art."

At noon I throw aside the rod because I have sighted a White Ensign, fluttering like a butterfly across the thin vista of sea that is visible from the stream. Focusing the glasses, I identify a Fishery Protection vessel; and for a fourth time Izaak Walton nudges my ear: "A debate hath arisen (and it remains yet unresolved) Whether the happiness of man on this earth doth consist more in Contemplation or action."

Ten minutes later I am frankly bored, not by the scenes, but by the rod that hinders a full enjoyment of them. Nor is the tedium eased when Walton resolves his debate between action and contemplation: "Both these meet together, and do most properly belong to the most honest, ingenuous, quiet, and harmless art of Angling."

Presently a farmer halts his pony, and calls across the meadow: "Any luck?"

"Not," I reply, "at the moment."

"You will. My little grand-daughter were down there yesterday, and her come back after an hour 'cause her got tired of hauling em in."

My fallen spirits re-arise when yet again Walton bids me stand fast, if only from an ulterior or non-piscatorial motive. Did not Walton say of a man "That he died. 13. Feb. 1601. being aged 95 years, 44 of which he had been Dean of St Pauls Church; and that his age had neither impair'd his hearing, nor dimm'd his eyes, nor weaken'd his memory, nor made any of the faculties of his mind weak or useless. 'Tis said that angling and temperance were great causes of these blessings. . . ."

But within a short while I am at it again, wishing that I were not fishing. Only a dedicated man may enter into the secret: "Cast the net on the right side of the ship, and ye shall find. They cast therefore, and now they were not able to draw it for the multitude of the fishes." On reflection, I had better forego casting, and take to a float which I can glance at now and again, between watching a goldcrest, or scanning the sea, or wondering how on earth to choose from among the uncountable topics which heap themselves like beneficent petals on the head of every man who writes of the countryside.

Then Walton plays his last card, his trump, his ace of aces: "I meet everywhere in this Country with these little Brooks, and they look as if they were full of Fish; have they not Trouts in them?" But this time he has spoken in vain. Gathering-up my rod, I set the fly alongside its other unavailing brethren in their glass box. It is as well, I think, that men no longer hunt for their supper. Nevertheless, the day was not in vain, for I have received the four blessings that were bestowed proxywise on Walton by his friend, Sir Henry Wootton:

> The showers were short, the weather mild,
> The morning fresh, the evening smiled.

8

Reaping the Years of Experience

The wheat turns yellow, and the year grows ripe. In country places men gaze over gates, or dawdle beside hedgerows, apparently unemployed. These are the farmers of Britain, who, so far from having nothing to do, now confront their most important task, the harvest. Why, then, should they appear idle? That is a misleading question because it assumes that farmers do appear idle, whereas any countryman knows that gate-gazing and hedge-dawdling are the farmer's surest way of deciding when a field must be reaped. It is a strange reflection, and one full of hope for mankind, that no machine at all can reckon the ripeness of wheat. Fortunately, a grain crop does not reach maturity and then lose it overnight. Farmers have a week or two in which to harvest well. Their astuteness is most keenly tried by bad weather. Is the crop really ready? Or must it bide awhile, taking its chance against the gales that may flatten it irreparably?

This ability to say on Monday "No", and on Wednesday "Yes" . . . how soon does a man acquire it? Not in one year; that I can say from experience as a farm pupil. Nor can it be acquired in two years. The course lasts for several seasons, and much of the tuition must come from the pupil himself while he compares his own verdict with that of lifelong experts. How is it done? It is done by gazing over those gates (quizzing the colour of the crop) and by dawdling beside those hedgerows (feeling the hardness of the grain). But if you ask me *how* the colour is quizzed, and *what* the grain tells the finger, I can say only that nobody knows. The thing appears to be an innate skill, made perfect by practice.

It has become fashionable to believe that the universe happened by Chance. What a coincidence, therefore, that the corn grows ripe predictably in late summer, never unpredictably in early spring or mid-winter. What a coincidence, too, that a root of wheat knows to by-pass a stone in its path, and to extract from the soil those ingredients which best nourish it. It used to be said that on the second day after sowing, the skin over an embryo seed breaks. On the third day a white spot appears, which becomes the tip of the radicle. On the fifth day the entire sheath is exposed, and from it the shoot and the root emerge. To start with, the shoot (or plumule) outstrips the root, but soon the root draws level as though—by Chance—it understood the plant's need of food and of a firm anchorage in the soil. Within a fortnight the plant is being nourished by five roots. Presently the leaves shake off their cotyledonous covering; and at the end of the first month a plant attains the form of its maturity. The rest lies with the gods, whom Richard Church trusted:

> Worship the summer sun
> In the high heavens burning,
> While the wheat-filled earth
> Ripens, slowly turning. . . .

Many people regard the harvest either as an archaic rite or as a mechanical process. Their progeny, no doubt, will suppose that bread grows in ovens, that milk is born in bottles, and that mackerel live in transparent bags. Bread meanwhile remains a staff of life. But what food-faddists we have become! For economy's sake the millers long ago discarded millstones, and took to metal rollers, which, by removing much of the nourishment, invite— nay, require—you to buy it back again, as yeast tablets, from the men to whom the millers had sold it. Concurrent with this 'economy' the price of bread has risen by four hundred per cent within a short lifetime. In all Britain there cannot be more than a few hundred people who regularly eat real bread and butter. I do know one Welshman who grinds his own corn, and then has it baked by his wife, who also churns butter; but those necessities cannot now be bought from even the most luxurious shop, though in our grandparents' childhood they formed part of the diet of many farmfolk. Today, by contrast, we remove the hygienic wrapper, spread the anaemic slice with diluted butter, and afterwards reach for an indigestion tablet. As Dr Hoskins declared, the average white loaf is "an obscene caricature of bread". Very different were the loaves which they baked when Celia Fiennes dined three centuries ago at "Corpus Christus Colledge". She found her portion "very good bread . . . remarkably the best. . . ."

Reaping becomes increasingly a mechanical process, and, having finished it, the machinists hurry home in another machine. So be it; there are things to be said both for and against the old methods and the new. In time, perhaps, our tractorised acres will yield a crop comparable with that taken by the horse-drawn peasants of the Dordogne Valley. But the poetry and the gratitude are dead. Never again, one feels, will English farmhands sing the chorus of R. D. Blackmore's *Exmoor Harvest-Song*:

> The wheat, oh the wheat, and the golden, golden wheat!
> Here's to the wheat, with the loaves upon the board!
> We've been reaping all the day, and we never will be beat,
> But fetch it all to mow-yard, and then we'll thank the Lord.

Those oldtime harvests did possess some merits. The cottagers liked to see the parson gird his cassock, and lead the way into the wheatfield. They liked to see their children gleaning for the hens. They liked to see the last stook safely gathered, head-high in triumph. They enjoyed the supper of beef and beer which the farmer provided gratis. They may have enjoyed the morrow's hangover, as part of the pageant. Such were the folk for whom Robert Stephen Hawker, eccentric vicar of Morwenston in Cornwall, invented what we now call the Harvest Festival service, by announcing that bread for the next Holy Communion would be baked from wheat harvested in a field near the church (the most northerly in Cornwall). Despite a cry of "Popery" the vicar lived to see his Harvest Festival become a national event alike in church and chapel.

Richard Jefferies said: "Every day something new is introduced into farming, and yet the old things are not driven out." But Jefferies wrote a hundred years ago. He has become an antique, like the handful of farmers who continue to spread their harvest supper, and the sprinkling of marvellers who continue to acknowledge an old miracle. Actors and spectators arrive by car, and are careful to depart in time for television. Some of the more thoughtful among them may remark, in passing, on the curious persistence with which Chance gives us this day our daily bread.

Show Business

They were at it when I passed by at suppertime. Three hours later, when I re-passed, they were still at it. In fact, they had been at it for a whole year . . . or, to be precise, for three hundred and sixty-four days, which is the time that elapsed between this year's show and last year's. And they really had been at it, beginning, as I say, last year when they sat amid the mud and the litter and the empty marquees while the chairman of the Show Committee—brown-booted and black-bowlered—turned to the sexton, who for thirty-seven years has been the show's sanitary inspector.

"Charon," he says (the nickname came from a classical curate), "next year thee mun rewrite it."

"Why?" asks Charon.

"Because," says chairman, "her ladyship said so."

"Why did she say. . . ."

"Because she's turned progressive."

"I don't see what the devil. . . ."

"Mr 'Obbs, she says to me, Times have marched, she says. The wind of change has caught us as you might say on the 'op. In other words, she says, thee mun take down *Ladies* and put up *Women*."

"But. . . ."

"Wait! Furthermore, she says, it would be nice if you was to place the tent a little further from the shooting gallery."

"But the ladies' women's tent has always been. . . ."

"Some of our marksmen, she says, gang a gurt way off't 'arget."

The casual holidaymaker, spending an hour at a country show, knows little of the hard labour that made his time pass pleasantly. The rent of the meadow, the value of prizes, cost of placards, order of precedence, quantity of refreshments . . . all must be assessed, settled, confirmed. But not everyone concurs. The owners of prize bulls will not accept responsibility if the brass band suddenly lets-go within a yard of the show ring. The rector will not address the proceedings if—as happened last year—his words are interrupted by the Refreshment Tent shouting: "Coom on't, lads. Git pissed for a penny!" The Hon. Miss Saddle will not judge the Fell ponies if Thwaite of Rigg Farm is allowed to compete (last year he was heard to call her "owd 'oss-face"). And sometimes an agonising reappraisal must be made: shall the show be opened by the baronet who has no money or by the businessman who has nothing else? The gravest problem—the weather—must be left to resolve itself; and again the spectators may not feel satisfied, for many of our country shows take place in autumn, a season whose "mellow fruitfulness" merges with the equinoctial gales. In Westmorland they use the phrase 'Brough weather' as a synonym for the snow, hail, sleet, mist, rain, and wind which too often mar that famous assemblage of gipsies and farmers and ponies.

Both Sir John Lubbock and Sir Henry Maine believed that fairs sprang up on sites which had been used as a no-man's-land where hostile communities might safely parley. Having become symbols of security, the sites were chosen as places of business because safety is a condition of commerce. The first of the mediaeval Statutes of Winchester took care to protect merchants, requiring each side of a highway to be cleared of bushes and trees to a depth of two hundred feet, so scorching the earth from under the feet of stealthy robbers. Even after the Reformation, shutters were shut at Sunday service time. Queen Elizabeth I decreed that "in all fairs and common markets, falling upon the Sunday, there shall be no showing of any wares before the service be done". Then, as now, the quality of commerce varied. Passing near Rye, Celia Fiennes reported: "Here was a faire which was rightly called Beggar-Hill Faire being the saddest faire I ever saw, ragged and tatter'd booths and people. . . ." In Shropshire, by contrast, she was impressed favourably: "From Shrewsbury I went through the great faire which was just kept that day there, full of all sorts of things and on all the roads for 10 mile at least I met the people and commoditys going to the faire. . . ." Three centuries later Mary Webb and her husband carried to Shrewsbury market the fruit and flowers which they grew on Lyth Hill:

> Who'll walk the fields with us to town,
> In an old coat and a faded gown?
> We take our roots and country sweets
> Where high walls shade the steep old streets. . . .

Country fairs have been well served by poets and others. Widecombe became as famous as Tom Pearce's old grey mare; Horncastle, once the premier horse fair in Britain, received a whole chapter from George Borrow; Delius set Brigg Fair to music; and from Thomas Hardy the cheerful Dorchester Fair received no less than seven mournful poems. Few fairs, however, retain more than the façade of their former importance. In the first volume of *A Tour Through the Whole Island of Great Britain*, which appeared in 1724, Defoe described Sturbridge Fair as

> not only the greatest in the whole nation, but in the world . . . the shops are placed in rows like streets, whereof one is call'd Cheapside; and here, as in several other streets, are all sorts of trades, who sell by retale, and who come principally from London with their goods; scarce any trades are omitted, goldsmiths, toyshops, brasiers, turners, milleners, haberdashers, hatters, mercers, drapers, pewtrers, china warehouses . . . with coffee-houses, taverns, brandy-shops, and eating-houses, innumerable, and all in tents, and booths. . . .

There is a sense in which the fairs have come full circle, because their name, *feria*, was the Latin for 'holiday' as opposed to a severely commercial occasion. And how the parish swells with pride whenever a neighbour takes the prize for pigs, or a rosette for the dog. It is drinks-all-round at the pub that night, and a rush for the next issue of the local newspaper.

And so we leave them as we found them, in the silent aftermath of another year's show, while the chairman turns to Charon, saying: "Next year happen thee mun put Swardles in't 'owd Bob's slack."

A Well-Beloved Physician

There were four of them, and their factory was filled with phones, files, and whitefrocked fillies. Presently a car drew up, and the plumber's wife emerged. Thrusting her head through the booking office, she exclaimed: "Got me biotics, luv?" A small package appeared. "Ta-a-lot. Cheery-bye." And so, with an audibly feminine gear change, Time motored on.

Inside the factory, however, Time remained unchanged despite the cushioned seats and their glossy magazines. Fear and pain sat

However, we cannot all be psycho-analysed when we develop a chill, or try to commit suicide by 'accidentally' falling into the machinery that is making our life intolerable. Where millions are concerned, a thousand alleviations seem of more worth than a hundred cures. All the same, there was much to be said in favour of the doctor who did know the names of his patients, some of whom he had delivered into the world, and vaccinated, and congratulated when he presented them with their own firstborn. Such a man belongs to that devoted company whom Balzac made famous in the person of Benassis, *Le Médecin de campagne*, whom the villagers called *Le bon Monsieur*, "the father of us all".

Playing it Cool

This was chalk country where springs abound, but rivers are rare. From a flawless sky the sun beat down as upon Wordsworth's Waggoner:

> The air, as in a lion's den,
> Is close and hot.

Seeking refuge from the glare, I remembered a hilltop pool, and straightway made toward it, through a meadow of Friesians and one Jersey whose task was to maintain the fat-content. Away to my right the land sloped steeply into a valley that re-arose on a skyline of amber wheat and milkwhite farms. Bright as a cherry, a combine-harvester stood at Action Stations, ready to reap. Ahead I saw the rampart of trees around the pool.

Several generations of farmers took pains to protect the place. First, they built a palisade of beech trees and three Scotch firs; then, by way of vallum, they set a well-staked wire fence. As a result, foxes and rabbits now share with insects and birds a benison that had been built for cattle and sheep. Coming in from the heat, I recalled that on my previous visit, in March, the path had been blocked by snow; now it was warm to touch, and stood knee-deep among ferns. But the place felt cool—that was the main thing—being shielded by trees and a hilltop breeze which turned itself on and off, like a bath tap. With eyes no longer screwed against the glare, I sat comfortably on the tomb of a tree whose

memory: "Don't hardly seem possible, do it? But 'tis true. Coal we got, and vegetables, and bananas. I remember they bananas particular 'cause some o' th'old folks hadn't never seen any afore. One old girl called 'em banners."

"How much did they cost?" I asked.

"How much? Now that I don't remember. But I'll tell 'ee one thing. You couldn't buy a single banana on its own."

"Why not?"

" 'Twas too cheap, that's why not. And I'll tell 'ee something else. If you'd gone down to the quay, and dumped a sovereign on the deck. . . ."

"You could have bought the whole cargo."

"Cargo? My dear soul, you could have had the bloody ship as well."

"How long ago was all this?"

"How long?" He glanced up at the sun. "That needs a slice of arithmetic." Then he called toward the kitchen: "Missus, how old am I?"

A head appeared at the window: "How what?"

"How old am I?"

"Too old, if you can't remember your own birthday."

"Come on, woman. Is it ninety-three or ninety-four?"

"Midway between the two. And by the sound of it you'm not likely to reach the second." The head disappeared.

"Call it ninety years, Sir."

"Eighteen seventy-nine."

"I dare say you'm right. But if you ever live to my age, you'll be timing yourself with a stopwatch. Anyway, we'd an old . . . and now I'm talking about modern times, mind . . . near enough the year nineteen-five . . . we'd an old smack . . . rerigged as a ketch she was . . . built in Cornwall in seventeen-eighty-seven. That's a date I do remember. The *Looe* they called her. The point is, that old lady was plying in and out o' Minehead this century. Ah, and she used to call once a year at a house . . . sounds strange, doesn't it? . . . house named Glenthorne."

"That's in a cove, surely, between here and Lynmouth?"

"Yere and Lynmouth," he nodded. "A parson lived at Glenthorne in them years. A Mr Halliday. And at high water th' old *Looe* beached herself with a cargo o' coals for 'en. And when her'd delivered to Glenthorne, she used to visit another cove . . .

K

we called 'en Embelley . . . and there she'd take-on a cargo o' pit-props for Wales."

"There were many sorts of cargo," I agreed.

"And that's another thing I remember." He leaned forward. "You've heard of a stage coach, no doubt?"

"Yes, indeed."

He examined my wrinkles: "You'm more than old enough to have ridden in 'en 'cause 'twas running till nineteen twenty-four. Six horses they had, to haul 'en out o' Lynmouth. And when they reached Countisbury . . . you know the Blue Ball? . . . well, that's where they slipped two o' the six." Again he quizzed me. "Are you getting fed-up with all this stale news?"

I shook my head, waiting while he rummaged his memory.

"You was asking about the cost o' bananas just now. Well, in my young days . . . no, dammit, right up to thirty years ago . . . you wouldn't find no self-respecting farmer ever paid his bills but once a year. Then he'd invite all his creditors, and give 'em a great beer-feast, and pay 'em one by one, cash down, for all the world to see. 'Tis very different nowadays. They deliver the bill afore they've delivered the goods."

And then he gave his verdict on past and present.

"'Tis no use trying to compare them. It was a different world. I loved it, mind, 'cause I was lucky in it, and young in it, and could ride the moor all day, and then fish the sea all night. But if you was unlucky, and getting on in years, well, then, I suppose 'tis better nowadays, with doctors round the corner, and the Voluntary Women to lend a hand when the river's flooded you out."

I rose to go, fearing that I might have overtaxed him; but already he was off again, on a new tack.

"About the year nineteen hundred I was courting a girl. Not," he glanced at the kitchen, "not the piece as eventually caught me, but another one, and she'd a brother who sailed in a ship called the *Friends*. Now she really was old . . . the ship, I mean, 'cause the girl can't ha' been above sixteen." A gentle smile compressed his furrows. " 'Tis coming back to me now. Appledore she belonged . . . the ship, you understand, 'cause the girl, bless her, she was born at Parracombe, daughter of a chap who went around saying his second cousin's brother wrote *Lorna Doone*. Or it may have been his brother's second cousin. Anyhow, that sailing ship was launched soon after the battle o' Waterloo."

9

Requiem for Summer

How swiftly summer wanes, and yet how slowly and with what poise. From end to end the kingdom is a quilt of cornfields that more than catch the eye; they so captivate it that country-folk lean on a gate, gazing at the golden prospect. But behind that prospect lurks another, for some of the southern harvest has been reaped, and in the north it is ready. The trees look tired. The grass turns brown. The sap recedes. Even the sun arises later and retires betimes. The world is a season older.

No man ages twice; his one-and-only experience of it is to him utterly novel despite the news thereof, which Sir Thomas Browne broke to himself: "The lives not only of men, but of commonwealths, and the whole world, run upon a circle, where, arriving at their meridian, they decline in obscurity, and fall under the horizon." Browne was an Anglican who looked beyond time, yet the autumnal mood prevails. *Partir*, said the Frenchman, *c'est mourir un peu*. When summer dies we live a little death. Many wise men, and a holocaust of fools, have prescribed remedies for that malaise. Yet some people seem never to suffer it, or, if they do, to be so slightly infected that the morrow finds them healed. I met such a man near Stanton St John, along the border between Oxfordshire and Buckinghamshire. Perched in a wayside garden, high above the lane, his brown wrinkles carved a perpetual smile. All around him the fruits and flowers of year-long labour spanned the spectrum fragrantly. Indoors his wife was putting a grandchild to bed.

"Another?" she exclaimed. "But you've 'ad three already, luv.

Even though oi did bake 'em, too many o' them cakes gives little boys a noightmare. Oi never used to let you mum 'ave mor'n three. Not at bedtoime oi didn't."

Hearing her, the old man smiled: "Oi were the same," he confessed. "Fact oi were wusser. Oi slipped down and stole the larder." He rubbed his rheumatism reminiscently: "Cor, 'ee didn't 'alf tan me, my 'ole dard." Then he glanced up at the sun, and down at the asters: "Still, a day loike this makes everything seem worthwhoile." Our intellect rejects that proposition, but the man who can accept it has already healed himself, and needs no other medicine.

Feeling at any rate none the worse for my own dose of it, I return to the car, and drive slowly on, westward into an evening whose shadows gape like ebony chasms on lawns that are greener than April. Seen against sunshine, the walls of a church turn black, and whitewashed cottages cease to gleam, though their flowers—caught in a pool of light—are glossier than the seedsman's catalogue. Scarecrowed in mid-field, one solitary elm casts a shadow that reaches to the farthest hedgerow, and then climbs it, sitting bolt upright on blackberries. At a crossroads two boys play one-a-side cricket while others speed the season with three-a-side soccer. Girls fidget near the signpost, wondering whether anything new will turn up. When it does—in a sports car—they stare awhile, and then resume their chatter; never still for an instant; always admiring a toecap, or tossing a braid, or turning aside to laugh.

Zig-zagging drunkenly into the sun, George cycles with one hand screening his eyes. Alighting with a wobble at the pub, he calls to the retired constable who is mowing his lawn across the way: "Pissed afore oi starts, eh?"

The constable smiles, but remembers his former duties:

"George!"

"Ah?"

"No rear red 'un."

"Not?" Amazed, George looks down at his machine, and then backwards along the lane: "Now where could thart ha' dropped orf?"

"Not where, George. When."

"But. . . ."

"Oi aren't see that light o'yourn this past week."

"Okay." George goes quietly. "Landlord'll lend me one."

"Oi 'ope so. Gits dark earlier these nights. Be good."

Emerging from a tin shack, where he has endured the heat and horseflies of the day, a superannuated hunter plods toward the gate as though, like the girls, he too has an eye for novelty. And there he waits, the portrait of patience, swishing his tail against a fly-by-night. Nor does he wait alone, for presently a tweed-jacket man joins me at the gate. An arm goes out to stroke the venerable mane.

"He was twenty-five last month."

"I wouldn't have thought it."

"True, though. We've both been over the sticks. And now," he pats the patient muzzle, "now we're both out to grass."

The Royal Horse Artilleryman raises his shooting stick, and with the tip of it straddles a fly that is exploring his left ear. He appears eager to talk, but I have a destination, so we agree that we may meet again one day.

This is sheepland as well as corn country, a frontier between stone and chalk, Cotswolds and Chilterns. Through the vale a scarlet combine ends the last journey of the day; and when silence returns, sheep enhance it from a hill. In the act of disappearing, the sun sets its mark halfway up one beech tree in a coppice, lurid as limelight on a sombre stage. Somewhere a robin sings, as though to mock the outmoded blackbird.

Now only the sunset remains, day going down like a fiery Temeraire. Hearing quiet footsteps, I turn, and there is Walter de la Mare's tangible vision:

> Softly along the road of evening,
> In a twilight dim with rose,
> Wrinkled with age, and drenched with dew,
> Old Nod, the shepherd, goes.

"Lovely evening."

" 'Tis an' all. Goodnight."

On, then, through tranquil pleasures amid places so far from the madding crowd that a rabbit squats beside the lane, lingering in the last light of summer's penultimate month.

Laissez-Faire

Sometimes even the wisest man speaks too soon. A century ago, for instance, Richard Jefferies wrote an obituary: "Gone," he lamented, "is the old-fashioned shopkeeper whose family had been tradesmen for generations, and waited in person, in his apron and black sleeves, upon his customers, or at least upon the better sort of them." As though he foresaw the serve-yourself shops that now reduce everyone to the most conspicuously common factor, Jefferies added a postscript: "Railways and co-operative stores have left no room for these shops." But Jefferies was too gloomy. During the Second World War a grocer at Great Missenden served always in a bowler hat and just such a black-sleeved apron as Jefferies had mentioned.

The old-fashioned shopkeepers are not dead. On the contrary, some of them prosper as never before, having been rescued from insolvency by "the better sort of customer" who, after all, does not pay a surgeon in order to be told "Sew up yourself." I know of one country town wherein a serve-yourself shop tried to compete with the old-fashioned kind. Said a local shopkeeper: "I'll give it a week." And he was right; and the customers, too, were right because their attitude reflected something more reasonable than cussed conservatism. In deep country, where women spend much of the day alone or with small children, a visit to the shops is an escape to wider skies. Such customers expect to gossip. Above all, they expect to be waited-on for a change. Nor are farm-wives the only people who decline to join the unsociably democratic queue. Men likewise appreciate service and an exchange of news. Certainly I have my own list of sociable shops, and will sometimes increase the cost of living by making a six-mile detour in order to buy one loaf of bread from an agreeable bakery.

It is in a village shop that you are most likely to meet the most old-fashionable kind of shopkeeper. The Ministry of Health might suggest some improvements to the premises, but the customers themselves require none. The first thing to greet you on entering is a door-bell which jangles so persistently that the echo drowns your request for a box of matches. The second greeting comes from a many-mingled aroma of cheese, boots, lavender,

fly-papers, peppermint, mops, coal-scuttles, envelopes, news-papers, seed cake, and paraffin. This display of wares is not more remarkable than the shopman's ability to weave a way among them. Thus, if you want tea, he finds it on top of corned beef, beside coffee; and if you want sugar, he finds that under the frying pans, alongside the weed killer. But even the shopman sometimes fails to hit the mark, or at any rate will put the mark in the wrong place. Thus, a card saying *Homegrown* (which belongs with the cucumbers) may find itself against a saucepan; and

another card, saying *New Laid*, will lie among the lemons. One card, however, seems never to be out of place; saying simply *Seasonable*, it appears on gardening gloves in spring, across deck-chairs in summer, between tulip bulbs in autumn, and among fire-lighters in winter. It is understandable that a commodity will sometimes (as we say) run-out; after many years it may run away, as it did from the sub-Post Office at Penuwch in Cardiganshire, where, on asking for a letter-card, I was told, after long search: "We did have one, but we've lost it."

It was during an interview with Colbert, in 1680, that another French economist, Legendre, exclaimed impatiently: *"Laissez-faire, laissez-faire!"* Several small traders have carried that economic policy into their private lives. I know one shopkeeper whose hours of business are from nine until six, but only when "Barkis is willing". That particular Barkis is sometimes unwilling, especially when the fish are rising in the stream nearby. At such times it is not unusual to find his shop shut despite an *Open* sign. The procedure is then as follows: the customer announces himself to the shopman's deaf sister who, after forty years' experience, knows whether her brother would wish to be disturbed. But as the deaf sister lives a quarter-mile uphill, it is often quicker either to go without or to visit a shop in the next village.

There are occasions when you discover that to come first is not always to be first served—nor indeed to be served at all—by the shop which reserves its six tins of tobacco for the vicar, who never smokes anything else. When you point out that the vicar is unlikely to purchase half-a-dozen tins at a time, you are reminded that you never can tell: to which there are either many answers or none at all, though Marx seemed to have had the shop in mind when, in the first volume of *Kapital*, he remarked: "A commodity seems a commonplace sort of thing, easily understood. Analysis shows, however, that it is a very queer thing indeed, full of metaphysical subtleties and theological whimsies."

A similar féy is sometimes seen hovering above the name of a shop. Near Truro in Cornwall there is, or recently was, a mobile fish shop called Sam and Nephew; and at Thame in Oxfordshire a furnishing shop is called Smith Sons and Daughters. Perhaps those large-family firms hope that the names of their relatives will inspire confidence, or maybe obtain custom by evoking pity for the Sons and Daughters and Cousins and Great-Aunts who must share the profits, and bear the losses. But the most optimistic tradesman I ever heard of was a farrier on the upper Thames, who, some sixty years ago, was called out to repair an aircraft that had landed nearby. Next day the roof of his forge bore an invitation in large white letters: *Aeroplanes Mended.*

The Green Roads

Lawyers of the constitutional kind will be able to decode the following cryptogram: *2 and 3 Philip and Mary. Cap. VIII.* Other people—myself among them—will need to be told that the cipher refers to a famous sixteenth century Statute, the first attempt by the central government to make and conserve our roads. Instinctively one imagines a metalled road; but the instinct is mistaken because in Tudor England and for at least two centuries thereafter all roads were green insofar as they had grass down the middle, and hedges on either side: pleasant indeed for strollers, but to serious travellers so hazardous that, long after the steam engine had been invented, coaches were still overturning, axle-deep in a wintry rut.

Edward Thomas was more fortunate, for he lived to savour the very heyday of our country roads, when they were so free from noise and death that nine-tenths of them had never seen a car. Rhyme merged with reason in Thomas's *confessio amantis*:

> I love roads:
> The goddesses that dwell
> Far along invisible
> Are my favourite gods.

No part of Britain holds a monopoly of green roads. You will find them on the Wiltshire Downs; sometimes as a Celtic track, sometimes as the remains of a metal surface which the Romans built over that track. In Norfolk the Peddars Way leads to the shores of the Wash; and you can walk along it for hours, over springy turf between hedges of wild rose, passing nothing more noisesome than the ruined priory at Castle Acre, which William de Warenne founded, as a cell of Lewes Priory, to repay the Cluny monks who had sheltered him and his wife during a pilgrimage to Rome. In the far north of Britain, across Perthshire, miles of green road show where the Legions marched through Caledonia.

In Shropshire once—only a mile from Church Stretton—I became so sickened by traffic that I climbed the nearest gate, and then strode at four miles an hour, following my nose until it was no longer affronted by fumes. Then I sat down to consult the map; and then I stood up again, almost at once, because the map assured me that a green road lay scarcely a hundred yards away. The map was right. Within a few moments I had reached the Roman Watling Street to Leintwardine. Soon the cacophony of cars dwindled to a drone, and was presently drowned by the birds.

You must move swiftly if you would travel the handful of green roads that are still in constant use, for Time marches on them with heavy tread. Only a year ago I set out to renew an old Westmorland acquaintance, the Galloway Gait or drovers' track which passes Kirkby Lonsdale *en route* for Scotland. While cars screeched into Lakeland, I would move leisurely over the fells, along a country lane with grass down the middle. Alas, I was mistaken. The grass had gone, and the Gait wore a new look, specially designed for lorries that were scarring the fells with a Motorway.

I sometimes think that the most impressive of my own green trackings occurred in the same county, near the hamlet of Knock, in a nebulous region known as Kirkland, under the lee of Alston Fell. Not even a map and compass will guarantee to discover that kind of road, because ploughs and tractors may obscure them overnight. However, after some tentative detours I did find the remains of the road which the Romans built, through a bleakly unpeopled country; a green road across the fells, steeper and incomparably straighter than the modern zig-zag from Hartside. Here and there the track was lined with stones that had been quarried and laid by Britons under the eye of a centurion. Still, after two thousand years, the line of their labours lay like an indelible shadow on the mountains, trodden deep by generations of natives who, when the Legions departed, continued to use the road, but lacked either the will or the skill to maintain it.

I remember, too, the Foss Way, which I followed on horseback from Lincoln to the Devon coast near Seaton. Among those who dwell beside it, the Foss is still the Old Straight Road, a monument to Roman engineers. Most of it is main road and therefore dangerously loud; parts of it are a country lane and therefore agreeably quiet; and in some places, where even the country lane has chosen to go its newer way, there the Foss becomes a green road, straight as the printer's die.

A road, said Hilaire Belloc, "is an instrument to facilitate the movement of man between two points upon the earth's surface". With that profound platitude the Romans agreed; wherefore their roads went straight, but never slavishly so. If a well-established track lay to hand, the Legions would sometimes follow it, bend or no bend, rather than build a more direct by-pass. You can see a vivid example of this in the West Riding, along the Roman road from Ingleton to Bainbridge, which indulges a good many curves while climbing Cam Fell and Dodd Hill, nearly two thousand feet above the sea.

The most pleasantly surprising green road in Britain is the Icknield Way, so-called (some say) because the Iceni first trod it, eastward from the Channel coast to the far west. There are traces of it near Royston in Hertfordshire, where it veers north from the Newmarket road. But the longest and loveliest tract lies in the Chiltern Hills, westward from Princes Risborough, where the high-banked Way ambles from Saunderton to the foot of Swyncombe Hill, within sight of Wittenham Clumps. Edward Thomas walked the whole Way, from the Gog-Magog Hills to the west country; and then he wrote a book about it, limp and weary as himself, a poet driven to prose in support of his family. But when the hack-work was finished, and he found in war the livelihood which peace had made elusive, then at last he spoke in his true tone of voice, confessing his love for the green roads, and what it had cost him to scribble a pittance from them:

> Often footsore, never
> Yet of the road weary,
> Though long and steep and dreary
> As it winds for ever.

A Yeoman of England

The house resembled the man, being hale, handsome, and furrowed by those invisible forces which transformed England from a farm to a factory. Seeing it, you half believed that, like the man himself, the place was too proud to mourn the past, and too wise to contradict the present. It had been made-to-measure, three centuries ago, for a yeoman. The word 'yeoman' originally meant a higher servant: "The king," wrote Sir Thomas Malory, "called upon his knights, squires, yeomen and pages." Later the word was used loosely to describe any kind of farmer, though more especially a freeholder immediately below the gentry. At the beginning of the nineteenth century those freeholders were the backbone of England, with the squires as ribs. Except during moments of aberration, when they were deluded by lawyers and other subversive merchandise, the yeomen stood foursquare to the winds of change. They were Tories, churchmen, more royal than the king, and some of them so utterly English that they never could quite believe that the French, too, possessed ploughs, and were able to write their own name.

Many great Englishmen came of yeomen stock: the Pastons, for example, who passed from yeomanry to gentility and thence into literature . . . Bishop Latimer, who burned for his faith ("Be of good cheer, Master Ridley, and play the man") . . . Thomas Bewick (his father combined farming with a one-man colliery in Northumberland), who rediscovered the art of engraving . . . William Cobbett, that Saxon-speaking defender of an old order against new disorder . . . Richard Jefferies, the voice of the open air. Both Jefferies and Cobbett disapproved the yeomen who were beginning to feel ashamed of their lineage. The yeoman's wife, said Cobbett, was "stuck up in a place called a *parlour* . . . a dinner brought in by a girl that is perhaps better 'educated' than she . . . the house too neat for a dirty-shoed carter to be allowed to come into". Seventy years later Jefferies was describing the final stages of that process when the daughters of prosperous yeomen employed their own 'lady's maid'. But we have wandered from the house.

It stands in the Cotswolds, on the edge of a hamlet, islanded among pastures and elms and sheep. I used to stay there during the 1930s, to ride the yeoman's horses. The man himself was a shade taller then, and his hair was brown, not white. By trade he was a grazier, selling carcasses to shops, and sirloins to housewives. There never were such sausages as his. They appeared by the trayful, thirty to each tray, and were devoured by a party of undergraduates and the agreeable young women with whom those gods still "fleet the time carelessly, as they did in the golden age". But again we have strayed from the house.

It has, if I remember, six bedrooms. My own (as I used to call it) was planked; and the planks were two feet wide. Day and night during winter a log fire leaped or dozed in a cavernous hearth with seats a-side, and a poker to mull your ale. No doubt they would call the paved kitchen cold nowadays, but we never found it so, for there also the temperature was warm and constant. Outside, a cobbled yard was flanked by aromatic barns and some looseboxes for the yeoman's hunters (one stallion had cost two hundred pounds, a princely price when value was sterling). The stable boy was a congenital jockey—short, freckled, bandy—attached permanently to straws which he wore in his hair like a cheerful and unshaven Ophelia. He served as a trooper in the Yeomanry. His name was Pete. And for a third time we have wandered off the premises.

Like Sir Christopher Wren, the old masons invite us to look around if we would see their monuments. This house is among those reminders; and its beauty has no necessary connection with the age of the beholder, for a young couple fell in love with the place, and lately bought it. The yeoman, now retired, continues nearby, in a smaller house.

A sporting peer of ancient lineage lived in the district, and some of his ancestors were buried in the church, but the yoeman's stock had preceded them thither by half a century. The yeoman was very proud of this. Of some other things he ought to have felt ashamed, assuming that you hold him responsible for them. Thus, we had what was then called a portable gramophone which we delighted to unleash classically by moonlight beside the garden pool:

> From harmony, from heavenly harmony,
> This universal frame began:
> From harmony to harmony
> Through all the compass of the notes it ran,
> The diapason closing full in Man.

At a little before midnight our own diapason was shattered by the yeoman shouting from his bedroom window: "Stop that bloody noise!" But against such flaws must be set many merits. We ourselves, for instance, could not quiz a hayfield and then say confidently: "Tomorrow I'll start mowing." We could not calm a stallion by standing still, and making soft chucks in our throat. Nor, when at last we climbed to the planked bedrooms, could we say, as the yeoman might have said with John Drinkwater:

> I turn to sleep, content that from my sires
> I draw the blood of England's midmost shires.

The yeoman's wife, a nice woman, insisted on sending the children to a 'private' school, but the husband felt no urge to keep up with anyone at all. He had been born-to-measure for the social order of his Edwardian childhood. That order has changed, and nothing foreseeable will revive its rights and wrongs. A mere thirty years have destroyed a countryside which seemed, like Traherne's corn, to abide "from everlasting to everlasting". Yet the new order bears traces of an honourable past. Not long ago I was in Cheshire, at the half-timbered home of a modern yeoman who has turned himself and his sons into a limited company, so that many kinds of machinery purr and sometimes shriek where once we crouched on stools beside a bucket in the byre. But the new man, too, is properly proud. His hearth is fiery, the roof raftered, the ale mulled. And from his twenty-horse-power steed he can still quiz a meadow: "Tomorrow I'll start mowing."

A Town and Country House

I have often thought how agreeable it must be to live in a small country town. Indeed, I would make my home there forthwith were it not that life long ago accustomed me to dwelling on a hill outside either town or village. I am therefore irrevocably with Robert Herrick who, from the depths of Devon, declared:

> We bless our fortune, when we see
> Our own beloved privacy.

Nevertheless, a small country town has its attractions. But how do you define such a place? Appleby, for example, is the capital of Westmorland, yet its population is only half of Prestwood's, which calls itself a village in Buckinghamshire. Again, St Asaph is a cathedral city, yet it remains smaller than Chinnor, which the Oxfordshire folk regard as a village.

In my own ideal country town the population does not exceed three thousand. That may suggest a village rather than a town, but if the maximum is exceeded, the spell will be broken by cinema, car parks, and modern architecture. Population, however, is only one of several yardsticks by which the genuine article may be identified; another is the market place; a third is the surrounding country which laps each end of the street.

I fancy that Britain's smallest country town is also a county town, Montgomery, an ancient royal borough with a population not much above nine hundred. Alone among Welsh towns, Montgomery had the good fortune to be rebuilt during the eighteenth century. It consists chiefly of Broad Street, which is a three-sided market square at the foot of Henry II's hilltop castle, now in ruins, but once the home of Lord Herbert of Chirbury and his clerical brother, George. Northward the Severn shines on its course from the summit of Plynlimon; eastward lies England, scarcely a mile away, lapping the Welsh meadows. Montgomery wears the *je ne sais quoi* which confirms that an apparent village is evidently a town.

Moffat, in Dumfriesshire, is larger than Montgomery, yet still a small place. It has a tree-lined river, a street both wide and High, and just enough by-ways to create an undoubted burgh. If you fell down dead in the middle of Piccadilly, millions of Londoners would neither know nor care; but in Moffat, when you sneeze, the news travels halfway to Selkirk: "So I said to him . . . you've no need o' the doctor. Take a wee dram, I said. It'll cost less and taste better. Aye, and it'll do more guid."

Cottagers still speak of "going to town" when they visit the shops at Middleton-in-Teesdale or Shipston-on-Stour. They may be said to use the General Theory of Relativity in a particular way. After all, if your own hamlet has one shop and ninety inhabitants, then Uppingham or Dunster will seem towns indeed, the very summit of hectic gaiety. And if you happen to live five miles along a mountain track, even the one-shop hamlet will acquire a metropolitan glamour. Thus, when I am living on Exmoor, miles from a village, the four shops at Parracombe create a kind of Regent Street, especially at Christmas, when the pork chops and toilet rolls are adorned with holly.

Moreover, even the smallest country town stands tiptoe on the stilts of its status. Those of us who are backwoodsmen feel impressed—almost dazzled—by the three gas lamps which announce night life in one country town of my acquaintance. We are apt to be misled by the luxury of having a brace of bakers, for competition seems less fierce than it used to be, and we no longer obtain a penny discount by inviting Town Bakeries to com-

L

pete with Oakroyd for our custom. However, we are still impressed by the Fire Station (just larger than its engine), by the Cottage Hospital ("Cheer up at once, all ye who enter here"), and by a brass plate announcing that the vet, the solicitor, and the chiropodist are to be found on Wednesday and Friday. One thing is certain; a small country town offers the best kind of shopping, like the tradesman in George Crabbe's Aldeburgh:

> William was kind and easy; he complied
> With all requests, or grieved when he denied.

Up-and-down seems the best description of the life of some country towns, as at Grampound, a Cornish village so unobtrusive that one of the lanes thither is too narrow for a wide car; yet Defoe reported: "Grampound is a market town and borough" (he might have added that it sent two members to Parliament). Or consider Derby, an industrial zone so vast that even the loop road looks interminable; yet Defoe reported: "Derby is a town of gentry, rather than trade."

Some towns declined so long ago that their heyday seems largely a matter of hearsay. It is four centuries since John Leland visited the tumbledown hamlet of Caersws near Llanidloes: "Poor Caersws," he sighed, "hath been a market and borough privileged." At Wroxeter you overhear the old Greek lamentation: "Being great, great was his fall" . . . for this small place was Uricon, the fourth city in Roman Britain. Standing amid her native corn, Mary Webb imagined the glory that was Rome:

> Still the ancient name rings on
> And brings, in the untrampled wheat,
> The tumult of a thousand feet.

Meantime, if you seek the country, but are reluctant wholly to lose the town, you may find your heart's delight at Beaminster in Dorset, at Lavenham in Suffolk, Wooler in Northumberland, Holt in Norfolk, Dulverton in Somerset, Hawes in Yorkshire, Bakewell in Derbyshire, Caistor in Lincolnshire, Oundle in Northamptonshire, Dartmouth in Devonshire, Kirkby Lonsdale in Westmorland, St David's in Pembrokeshire, Sutton Valence in Kent, St Just in Cornwall, Malmesbury in Wiltshire, Bampton in Oxfordshire, Oakham in Rutland, Rye in Sussex, Cockermouth in Cumberland, Ulverston in Lancashire. The best of those places are shapely as well as friendly. Their silhouette is fringed with fields; their streets, flecked with straw. Above all, they retain an iota of remoteness. At early morning, or when night has closed the last pub, they wear that faraway look which Robert Bridges etched with seven words:

> Eastward from Ida, in a little town.

By the Fireside

September is the time when firelight becomes the best cure for frostbite, though the precise moment of application will vary with the region. Among the South Hams of Devonshire, where frost is always late, a mellow Michaelmas can make firelight appear merely ornamental; but if you climb Cross Fell, and gaze over the Eden Valley toward Appleby, you will notice that every chimney wears a plume. Granted, there are evenings—and mornings, too— when June itself invites you to warm your spirits and your fingers by the fire. But those are *ad hoc* occasions, swept aside and thereafter forgotten until, as I say, a time comes for lighting the first of many fires.

In my own regions we still observe the ritual of log fires. Our wisest virgins may be seen wooding in high summer. I know of one Exmoor man who never returns from his walk without he brings a fallen bough, or some sticks for kindling. Elderly cottagers push prams into a Chiltern beech wood, returning therefrom so highly laden that they must either pull their push-carts or else steer by the very deadest reckoning. In return for an annual payment of one shilling to the late Earl's agent, the people of Prestwood and Great Hampden were allowed to collect any amount of fallen wood—without, however, causing it to fall.

Meanwhile the lighting of autumn's first fire becomes almost a sacrificial rite. Even the posture is reverent, on its knees. The mere act of handling wood seems strange after so many months; the hearth itself seems strange, being dusty and scarred. If you are idle, you prod your matchstick among mouldy newspaper and damp twigs, and then wait sullenly while a few sparks nibble the edge of last year's leading article. There is indeed such a thing as smoke without flames. If, however, you were brought up on firelight, and have lived all your days by it, then the paper is dry, the twigs brittle, the logs laced lattice-wise so that air may circulate freely.

Now comes the great moment. You strike your match, tilt it a little, and then draw it slowly across the paper. At once the lowermost twigs catch and crackle. An incense of blue smoke arises, mystic as the Indian rope trick. By this time the bark of the beech logs is ablaze. Still kneeling, you stare at a scarlet pattern flecked with yellow. Forgetful of fire's cruel aspect—the martyr at the stake, a forest in cinders—you surrender yourself to its vivid beneficence. Nor are you alone with your rapture. The rafters quiver in an ecstasy of light and shade. Bookshelves beget rainbows. The dog sits with both forepaws in the hearth, as though regretting the lack of a spit, on which he might toast all parts of his person. Cats pose a quiescent question-mark against the fender.

At last the fire is under way. Eddies of warmth reach you, invisibly potent like scent; and having shed their bark, the beech logs distil their own attar. Some say that apple is the most fragrant; others prefer cherrywood; but all agree that ash is the prince of fire-lighters. You can plunge an ash-bough into a bucket of water, and still it will blaze when the match is applied. If ash is the prince of lighters, then oak is the king of burners. Some old sailors feel sacrilegious when they burn oak. It is like razing the homes of the men whom David Garrick saluted:

> Heart of oak are our ships,
> Heart of oak are our men:
> We always are ready;
> Steady, boys, steady. . . .

In some parts of Britain the supply of coal is so near, and a dearth of trees so marked, that log fires become a rich man's extravagance. Elsewhere the people may live far from either timber or coal. In Sutherland the double-dearth is mitigated by a small private colliery at Brora; but crofters rely on their peat. When last I was at John o' Groat's the watermiller loaded the boot of my car with some of his own peat; and for the past two years I have burned a slice on the season's first fire. One whiff returns me to Caithness, that self-sufficient land, which the ancients called the Edge of the World. Just so, you remember, Marcel Proust recovered times past when he tasted a certain kind of cake.

In some country houses the first fire burns until the last. From September until April an alp of ash is rekindled each morning with a fistful of twigs. If you scatter that ash on the soil, the flowers in their season will rise phoenix-fashion from a wintry pyre. They say that the Duke of Buckingham and Chandos burned whole trees at Stowe House, such was the size of its largest hearth. The finest fires I know of are lit by two hotels, the Castle at Lydford on Dartmoor, and the Hunter's Inn near Parracombe on Exmoor. In those hostelries the 'log' is a courtesy title for half a tree. I tried using an open hearth myself years ago, but found that I gave more time to collecting and sawing logs than to sitting in front of them; when I compromised, by purchasing logs, I found that I was spending more money on them than on food; so, a less cavernous hearth was installed, and one foot of beechwood fits it nicely.

Even a small log is worth watching, as Richard Jefferies knew: "The bark of beech," he discovered, "is itself a panel to study, spotted with velvet moss brown-green, made grey with close-grown lichen, stained with its own hues of growth, and tinted by time." Yet you need not burn a tree in order to watch it blaze, for now is the time when the woods wear classical clothes, *flammantia moenia mundi*, "the flaming ramparts of the world".

I find it sad that to most people these ruminations will sound like the tales of a grandfather. Modern man presses the switch, and nothing happens except heat; no crackling companionship, no shadows on the ceiling, neither scent nor sound. Still, the old ways die hard among hardy old people, and at Withypool the other night I saw what John Clare noticed near Northampton long ago:

> The shutter closed, the lamp alight,
> The faggot chopped and burning bright,
> The shepherd from his labour free,
> Dancing his children on his knee.

10

The Voice of Autumn

Unlike March month, October comes in as a lamb, and departs to a whirlwind of leaves. It is as though the earth just now were resting between harvest and ploughing. The rest itself is brief because a shorn field lies naked to the sun and air that speed the weeds which, unless they are harrowed, will multiply. Farmers therefore pounce quickly. Sometimes they burn their stubble, which is cheaper than ploughing, and more profitable because it spreads a cindery dressing. In moorland country the heather, too, is swaled, and the smoke-scent emphasises a general stillness, which is not absence of sound, but a symphony of many sounds. Visitors from a town exclaim: "How silent it is!" Silence or noise . . . they have no other response, being so accustomed to noise that they carry the rumble with them, and its echo stifles stillness. Ears less sophisticated are more acute. Through his open window a countryman hears the sheep bleating, birds singing, hens cackling, streams flowing. Yet profound stillness has become a rarity. In ten seconds one aircraft disturbs a million people; main roads echo across the miles; motor-mowers intrude upon a village; machinery makes a farmyard sound like a factory.

How absurd it is—one may truly say, how insane—that stillness should be regarded as the voice of death instead of as the sound of life, which is seldom loud. Have you ever heard the grass growing? Or sap rising? Or your own tissues being born? Have you heard the Earth spinning on its axis? Or the conception of an idea? Yet those are the forms of life that deserve to be spelt with a capital L. It would be interesting to pursue the matter, onto those

heights where deaf Beethoven discovered his last quartets, and so
fulfilled the words of the prophet who said: "Be still, and know
that I am God." But few of us would choose to live as Trappists,
wrapped in the rags of our own rumination. We have a living to
earn. We are endowed with a temperament that demands a less
rarefied atmosphere. We are content to breathe Mary Webb's
Shropshire air: "When you lean from your bedroom window,"
she wrote, "into the silence of a country night, you are not at
first aware of it. It is like an invisible, enclosing bowl, and you

become aware of its depth only when a fox's bark rings in it like
a sharp silver thing. . . ." In deep country that boon abides
despite the times. A. E. Housman set the quietest places under the
sun among the Welsh Marches. Others find them on the Cheviots,
in the Scottish Highlands, among the vast undevelopment of
Caithness, beside the Severn above Newtown, and throughout
the Mendip Hills.

Deep or shallow, most country places receive the gift of
autumn stillness; and above it one bird comes into his own.

Though he is out-sung by linnets and larks, the robin has won the affection of poets. Herrick called him the "sweet-warbling Choirester". William Cowper, a lonely man, admired the bird's ability to be "pleased with his solitude". Blake anathematised those who ill-treat the bird:

> A robin-redbreast in a cage
> Puts all Heaven in a rage.

Robins have inspired some beautiful legends. Three centuries ago John Hoskins remembered that a robin's breast was red because the bird had tended Christ on the cross, plucking from the crown one thorn "to soothe the dear Redeemer's throbbing head". Izaak Walton declared that a robin "loves mankind both alive and dead". Michael Drayton was more specific when he said that robins perform humanity's last rites:

> Covering with moss the dead's unclosèd eye,
> The little redbreast teacheth charitie.

Emily Dickinson warned us not to underestimate the robin's artistry:

> Touch lightly nature's sweet guitar
> Unless thou knowest the tune,
> Or every bird will point at thee
> That wert a bard too soon.

John Clare liked to watch the October robin "tutling" or tootling among the season's berries. A rare critic was Gilbert White, who complained because the bird does "much mischief in gardens to the summer-fruits". Walter de la Mare, by contrast, greeted the robin as a friendly visitor "calling on all". W. H. Davies matched the bird's song with one of his own:

> How he sings for joy this morn!
> How his breast doth pant and glow!
> Look you how he stands and sings,
> Halfway up his legs in snow!

Ornithologists assure us that the robin sings a war-song in defence of his territory. Dangle a stuffed robin, they say, and the real robin will react as a bull to a rag. We must accept what Science has proved. But was ever aggression so sweetly expressed? And is hatred the song's only impulse—assuming that birds are something other than bundles of unemotive reflex? Strange indeed, that a creature so violent should appear so friendly. Who has not weeded his garden while a robin sat on the handle of the spade, or watched from a bough three feet away? Robin redbreast is the loyalest of our hardy perennials. Blackbirds fall dumb, and missel-thrushes await a storm, but the robin sings through fair and foul. I see him now—and hear him, too—as he perches like an outsize berry on the reddening mountain ash. His song is as gay as the birth of a beck. For all I know he sang there last October, and in November pecked at the windowpane as though to remind me that it was colder without than within. Certainly he seems to recognise me, or, more accurately, to show no sign of fear. When I went out an hour ago to stake the chrysanthemums after heavy rain, the bird positively got in my way. Already he has added his married man's mite to my own cost of living. Yet he earns every crumb, for when Michaelmas has gone, and summer with it, then comes the robin, and we know that he will remain with us, our fellow-traveller through the snow. It was a man from the snow—Wordsworth himself—who wrote six poems to this warlike ally, calling him "the bird whom men love best. . . . Our little English robin".

Shepherd's Pie

At four o'clock, as I was walking the Peeblesshire hills, I saw a shepherd on the skyline, with a crook in his hand, and a collie at his heel. And then, just as suddenly, the shepherd disappeared, but returned two minutes later, driving a Land-Rover as Jehu skidded his chariot. I hailed him, and he halted.

"Time marches on," I observed.

"Eh?"

"I see you travel by car."

"Mon, you no' think I've time to walk?"

And away he went, bumping over a bare moor.

Mind you, there is nothing amiss with shepherds who ride. On Exmoor and Dartmoor, and in parts of Wales, they still do use a pony; and in Lakeland, too, where they hold a soirée unknown among southrons. Imagine, then, a skyful of mountains, strewn with sheep. Then imagine a lane, draped like a thread of cotton, rising and falling among those mountains; and beside the lane a beck that boils over waterfalls. Finally, imagine a squat stone building—a pub, in fact—set back from the lane, apparently the only house in all the world. At such a place the shepherds and the sheep farmers foregather once a year, which is why the occasion is called a Shepherds' Meet.

It is true, of course, that telephones and newspapers have outdated the original purpose of the Meet, which was to exchange news of sheep in general and of a neighbour's strays in particular. Even so, the Shepherds' Meet remains something more than an excuse for a blow-out. Nor is it wholly a masculine event. On the contrary, the ladies appear and are the power behind the Shepherds' Pie, which is a collective noun, incorporating a whole sheep, two sacks of potatoes, an apple tart unlimited, buckets of tea, mountains of bread, whiskey galore, and all those other ingredients whose recipe was handed down from mother to daughter by way of priceless dowry. Chairs bring in the ratio of one to every ten visitors, most of the men lean or squat, warmed by a blaze that seems less a log fire than a conflagration of tree-trunks, daubing the rafters with kindly scars. Most of the guests arrive by car or motor-cycle, but some have come on foot, and a few will stable their ponies in the byre. Like all mountain people, they do not run out of their way to embrace strangers; but to them I am not wholly strange, for I spend a part of each year among them, and my name alone announces that theirs was the land of my fathers.

The company itself is mixed. A blacksmith will certainly look in, and perhaps his lordship's agent. The young rector always stands himself a pint of ginger-beer; travellers in foodstuffs arrive, combining business with beer; one or two hikers appear, attired like astronauts whose vehicle has broken down. From time to time a pretty girl glides through the tobacco smoke, bringing fresh sandwiches, or removing stale beer. Nature being as human as ever it was, the damsel receives unsolicited testimonials to several parts of her person, but never in a way to offend her father and her fiancé, who are discussing our native breed, the hardy Herdwicks: "Happen th'owd bitch got herself in't mud beyond Jamie's beck. 'Thee mun gang thine own way,' I shouted. Come suppertime, though, she were back agin wi' her lamb."

The humour is in every sense good. One farmer, aged seventy-eight, will greet another, aged seventy-nine, with: "Eest still alive?" Not long ago a professor on holiday hereabouts was asked by a farm-hand to open the gate for his sheep. The professor, however, failed to understand a word the man was shouting. At the Shepherds' Meet the man himself said: "Professor or not, I think nowt on him. I 'ollered 'Erpen thart gay-urt' and he never."

Though it will veer and back among politics and football, the talk seldom stays far from sheep, and is always dominated by them. Indeed, there are times when the shepherds seem to resemble their flocks. I have seen an old Herdwick, laden with fleece, wobbling wearily on matchstick legs; and next moment, alarmed by my dog, the ram had scaled ten feet of rock with the agility of a fawn. Twenty yards on, I met the shepherd, bent under a shawl of sacking, apparently in the last stages of senility; but when he reached a wall he leaped over it, scorning to unlatch the gate. He was the man to whom Vergil talked business:

> If woolgrowing is your trade, beware of prickly plants,
> Goose grass and star-thistle; avoid pasture that is too lush.
> Build on a white and soft-fleeced flock.

Down south they fold their hands, and cry that Socialism has corrupted the kingdom. They are wrong. At the Shepherds' Meet the farmers do not believe that every milkman ought *ex officio* to become a member of the Milk Marketing Board. As one of them put it: "Soon thee mun axe shape" . . . which being translated means, "We'll soon have to ask the sheep how to run our business." One agitator did come up, at somebody else's expense, but they cooled him off head-first in a waterbutt. These are the men whom Wordsworth described as: "A community of shepherds and agriculturalists, proprietors, for the most part, of the lands they occupied and cultivated." In the old days they were called Estatesmen, and at a Shepherds' Meet you can overhear their declaration of independence. You can, also, observe the astonishment with which that independence is regarded by shop-stewarded tourists from northern factories. They cannot place it. Some would like to call it Toryism, but are deterred by the knowledge that at lambing time many fell farmers work a ninety-hour week, and that the brief holiday without pay occurs once in five years. If a stranger does repeat the latest patois of politicians and other

orators, he will very soon be told: "Thee's nobbut a poll parrot."
A Shepherds' Meet is not the place at which to throw any sort of
weight about, if only because it will be caught and cast back by a
Lakeland wrestler. Up here it is the natives who have the last
laugh . . . at the townsman's genius for getting lost on mountains,
at his inability to tell Leicesters from Longwools, his habit of
taking the car out whenever he wants to walk ten miles, his flair
for falling down dead before he is fifty.

A Bronze Age

Autumn goes down like a Temeraire with colours flying, and the
ensigns are never so vivid as during the first days of November,
when frost has burnished their brightness. Though we speak of
autumn colouring, we ought really to call it discolouring because
green is the shade of a leaf until old age assails it. Like men themselves, leaves are as young as their arteries. In autumn, for
example, a layer of cork constricts part of the leaf-stalk and stem;
the green pigments are replaced by yellow or brown, and the last
link with the twig is severed, leaving a scar that is covered by skin
so that no parasitic spores can enter the wound. Because the
branches of a tree are more or less the same length as its roots, the
leaves lie where their decay is most likely to do most good,
immediately above the roots that are already feeding next year's
foliage. I know of one wood that is visited each autumn by a Rolls-
Royce whose owner and his chauffeur emerge with two sacks, and
then disappear among the trees, like a pair of body-snatchers.
Hearing them, the birds squawk, and every squirrel scurries upstairs into the attic. Ten minutes later the visitors re-appear,
staggering under their swag of leaf mould.

Said Richard Jefferies: "There are broken bits of summer to be
found in the fields far on into the shortening days." There are
indeed, yet autumn has no need of a discarded glory. It is ripe in
its own right. Country lanes are lined with hazel nuts, with hips
and haws, with the holly berries that at Christmas will blaze like
little bonfires. Rustling through the wood, ankle-deep in leaves,
you notice the acorns that admirals used to sow for future fleets,
not foreseeing an era of ironclads. Away on the hills, how swiftly
the winter wheat grows up. Swallows and house-martins have

departed; but redwings and field-fares arrive; and among the
fallen leaves you may share Dorothy Wordsworth's discovery:
"Wytheburn looked very wintry, but yet there was a foxglove
blossoming by the roadside."

In the end, however, it is the trees that steal a picture bright as
Swinburne's:

> The colour of the leaves was more
> Like stems of yellow corn that grow
> Through all the gold June meadow's floor.

The cherry leaf is scarlet; oaks, like old parchment; the beech,
as in a bronze age. Beechwoods, indeed, are the most flamboyant
of all the autumnal sights, though it was not for their colours that
Queen Elizabeth protected them against industrial axemen.
According to Thomas Fuller, the Queen decreed that no beeches
"being one foot square at the stub, and growing within fourteen
miles of the sea, should be converted into coal or fuel . . .". There
is a notable array of beech on the road between Cirencester and
Tetbury, not a great way from the source of the Thames. But the
tree shows at its best on chalk hills. Time has not withered the
infinite variety which John Davidson admired above Chequers
Court: "The Chilterns," he declared, "are famous for their
beeches; none are finer than those on this estate." Fiona Macleod
emphasised the need for a bright background to the leaves: "The
most subtle charm of the woods in November is in those blue
spaces which lie at so brief a distance in every avenue of meeting
boughs. . . ." When sky and water are blue, a voyage along the
Thames from Marlow to Henley burns itself into the memory.
Port and starboard the horizon catches fire, and in places only the
river itself can quench the flames. From the Oxfordshire Chilterns
at Ipsden, you look onto the roof of a manor house where Charles
Reade lived, among hills so high that not even their beech logs
could warm the cloister of his hearth: "The coldest house",
Reade called it, "in all Europe."

Other artists—including some of the giants—could not see the
trees for the wood which they had projected thereon. Charles
Dickens confessed that he found autumn "almost unbearably
depressing, a time of visible decay and protracted death . . .
altogether most horrible". In October the rustic Constable for-
sook his beloved Suffolk, preferring to spend the season in Lon-

don because he could not bear to witness what he called "the rotting melancholy dissolution of the trees". Shakespeare was neither the first nor the last lover who cursed his bald pate:

> That time of year thou mayest in me behold
> When yellow leaves, or none, or few do hang. . . .

Although she acknowledged it as the rebeginning of a cycle, Mary Webb saw also the season's sadness: "Autumn" she sighed, "is full of leave-takings." October stands fullsquare against those private storms; for Earth has no moods, and we ourselves dictate the message which the months recite. We have all been happy in an autumn deluge, and miserable in the summer sun.

Like the harvest, autumn catches the eye wherever it travels. My own lawful occasions lately led me through the Quantocks and Cotswolds to the Brecon Beacons and thence to St David's in Pembrokeshire; and all the while, from each hedgerow and every deciduous tree, a brown carpet was laid down in royal welcome. Yet this embrowned month offers something more than a study in aesthetics, for when I go to the porch, and listen intently, I hear the music of a saw from the valley where someone is warming himself in the act of preparing to do so. If the wood is apple or beech he will enjoy a fragrant fireside this evening.

Dazzled by October's spectrum, the poets have neglected somewhat the scent of its firewood, both indoors and out. An exception was Edward Thomas, who lived much among Le Gallienne's "shepherds and out-of-doors men"; digging his garden one autumn day, Thomas leaned on the spade, savouring October's colouring and

> The smoke's smell, too,
> Flowing from where a bonfire burns
> The dead, the waste, the dangerous,
> And all to sweetness turns.

So, like the falling leaves, a tree at its going-down outshines even the splendour of April, for is any sight more vivid than a bonfire?

In the Rough

I had seen better guns and costlier dogs, but never such a display of gun-doggery. Admittedly I was biased because the dogs and the gun were mine. Grousemen and gamekeepers will dismiss such very rough shooting as child's play, yet I enjoyed it, and found it worth doing, which is as good as most motives in an imperfect world. The procedure was—roughly—as follows: having taken a gun and a pocketful of cartridges, I would summon the terrier (named Bill) and the setter (named Red). Since the garden has neither a hedge nor a fence, we simply stepped out of it, crossed the cart-track, and entered a meadow which slopes steeply from the brow of a hill that used to bear corn, and then for a while was given over to beehives. Now it is a tangled no-man's-land where horses sometimes graze. But back to business: Bill would plunge into a minefield of bracken and briar under the hedge while Red stood frozen, a dozen yards away. After much rustling, I would hear Bill yapping invisibly. Then, more often than not, a rabbit emerged. If I missed, which I frequently did, Red would catch the rabbit by cutting off its retreat. To borrow of another field sport—Bill was the hooker, Red played scrum-half, and I served as participating referee. The results were not likely to impress the kind of guns which Burns depicted:

> The thundering guns are heard on every side,
> The wounded coveys, reeling, scatter wide.

Even so, I would emphasise two features of this very rough shooting. First, the dogs' intuitive teamwork; for Bill never pursued what he had put up, and Red never interferred with Bill's up-putting. Even more remarkable, Red—a setter—acted as a Saluki. I never trained the dogs to their division of labour. Now I come to think of it, I cannot recall when they first practised it. I know only that one morning they did practise it, and continued thereafter so perfectly that they usually hooked what I had failed to hit.

Some people will be dismayed when I confess that nowadays I dislike killing except in defence of human well-being. Even as a youngster I never carried a gun unless a rabbit were required for the pot, or its skin to line the fireside rug. But that does not set me among the anti-blood-sportsmen, who, if they were logical, would, like the Jains, wear a mask lest they inadvertently swallowed a gnat. Man, after all, was born a hunter, and every good marksman kills clean and quick. Nature's teeth and claws return a blood-stained answer to anyone seeking moral precepts. At best, some men must kill, or starve; at worst, others can divert onto rabbits and pheasants an instinct that might otherwise declare war overseas, or in the home. Though I admire Schweitzer's "reverence for life", I suspect the man who will neither swipe a wasp nor down a wolf. Above all, I despise the man who exploits field sports as a weapon in his own out-dated class warfare. Neither rough shooting nor fox-hunting ever was a prerogative of privilege: the former belongs to any lad with an air gun; the latter is permitted and subsidised by farmers and others of the middling sort, who form the greatest part of any Hunt in deep country beyond the Shires. Many of them follow in cap and rat-catcher jacket; most speak the music of their county; and every one of them looks down his nose at a snob. Vets now lead the field; and so do spinsters whose income is less than an overtime carsprayer's. The anti-sportsmen, in short, will receive more respect —or at least will appear more consistent—when they start throwing nails into a prize fighting ring, or acid on the trout stream. Isaiah, one feels, spoke in metaphors when he said: "The wolf also shall dwell with the lamb, and the leopard shall lie down with the kid. . . . They shall not hurt nor destroy in all my holy mountain. . . ." Britain has outgrown bear-baiting and cock-fighting; but not even the House of Commons can alter the nature of the majority of countryfolk, who love to chase the fox and to shoot a rabbit. That fact of life is too often ignored by people whose sensitivity does not allow them to follow such pursuits. To classify every field sportsman as a sadist is to play with words and to reveal the shallowness of one's knowledge of human nature. A man can be a good husband and kind father, yet still enjoy wandering with a gun under his arm. Some of my own best shooting days returned empty-handed. One or two did not fire a shot.

The increasing number of weekend sportsmen suggests that some are more likely to maim themselves than to kill their quarry. Only the other day I happened to enter a gunsmith's shop while

M

a visitor from London was sampling the second-hand wares. "What," he asked, "are these guns like?"

The dealer, being an honest man, replied that second-hand guns, like new ones, are lethal and probably more so. Buying an old weapon can become as dangerous as buying an old car. The riskiest kind of customer is attracted solely by the gun's appearance (especially by its stock). Others, less inexpert, examine the weapon's action. But if one part of a gun may be accounted more important than the rest, it is the barrel, which you can inspect by

holding it up to a bright light that will cast shadows down the bore. Some distortion of those shadows is allowable, and can be cured or 'raised' by a gunsmith; but a bulging barrel is not allowable, because its fatigued metal may explode. There is a manslaughterous undertone in the weapon which Edmund Spenser described:

> With windy mitre and quick sulphur fraught,
> And rammed with bollett round, ordained to kill. . . .

If I were buying a second-hand gun I would safeguard myself—

and my companions—in one or both of two ways. First, I would invite the dealer to examine the bores (and if he had no barrel gauges, I would regard him as a mechanic who practised without a tool-kit). Second, I might send the gun to be vetted at a proof house, assuming always that it was 'viewable' or in reasonably good condition, for no proof house will assess an out-worn weapon. The second is the surest way of testing a gun. The Worshipful Company of London Gunmakers has been doing it for three centuries.

Devonshire Cream with Roses

No one excels a countryman's flair for combining business with pleasure; nor is that combination anywhere more harmonious than at Bampton Fair, the reddest of Exmoor's red-letter days, made even brighter by the bracken and the berries of October. I feel an especial fondness for Bampton, partly because it has a streetful of Georgian houses, and partly because my ancestors lived there while those houses were being built. To city folk the place will seem no larger than a village, but on Exmoor it is rated as a town.

Bampton Fair—first licensed by King Henry III—has for long been another name for the annual sale of Exmoor ponies. The phrase "Wild West" utters an English timbre indeed when those frisky creatures are driven into town. Like the red deer, our ponies are indigenous and indomitable. Mediaeval kings tried to destroy them lest their small stature spread, and thereby imperilled the supply of armour-plated weight-carriers; Victorian business-men wished to sell the whole herd for cash; but always the ponies prevailed. Now they are protected by the Exmoor Pony Society, which keeps a stud book, and will not accept any animal unless it fulfils precise conditions. Thus, both the sire and dam must have been entered in the stud book; the pony itself must have been inspected and branded by the society; and mares may not stand above twelve hands, two inches.

In 1887 *Murray's Magazine* described Bampton Fair: "From end to end the long village street was blocked with horses and cattle, with sheep and with men." Then came a postscript: "Not a woman was to be seen . . . an unwritten law appears to prescribe

that in the morning the women shall keep out of the way." Today
the women arrive early, having driven a horsebox over the moor.
Their daughters win rosettes, and can handle six foals with a
verve that would have pleased Sabine Baring-Gould, who said:
"Let a visitor go to Bampton Fair, and see the pranks of these
wild and beautiful ponies, and note well the skill with which they
are handled by the men experienced in dealing with them." Wild
and beautiful indeed: wild because many of them roam the moor;
and beautiful because of their meal-coloured mouth, the broad
forehead, the dilated nostrils.

On fair day Bampton bulges. Cars and looseboxes are crammed
into meadows or squeezed among by-ways in the town. The High
Street becomes a tangle of stalls, booths, pedlars. If any motorist
tries to penetrate the crowds, he must proceed at their own pace,
not at his. It is fascinating to quiz the moorfolk as they spill from
the bar into the gutter, or drape their muddy legs around a table
at the café. The auctioneers are there, something between a
tipster and the late Sir Walter Gilbey. The *North Devon Journal* is
there, accompanied by notebook. Some clergy are there, some
doctors, some shopkeepers, a few autumnal holidaymakers, and
one person whose attire looks so aggressively horsey that you feel
certain he is safer on a pushbike.

The junketings are not a canned cacophony, but they do provide
a forum for many kinds of oratory. One shepherd remarks to
another: "There ain't no difference between 'em, that's what I
say. Whoever you vote for, the price o' wool goes down and the
cost o' beer goes up. And 'tis no use knocking their heads together 'cause even if you did you wouldn't get nothing but a load
o' sawdust."

But it is the farmers who steal the picture at Bampton Fair; the
working farmers, the married men, who have inherited an expertise which many a Bachelor of Science never will acquire. Their
complexion was long ago rinsed and rasped into a perennial tan.
Most of them are capped, and wear a macintosh—not the skimpy
modern sort, but a real swashbuckling garment, covering the
calves, defying even an Exmoor deluge. Nearly every man carries
an ash stick. Briar pipes seem to grow spontaneously, like ad-
ventitious teeth; and the soles of boots are as thick as sponge-
cake. A farmer's good humour makes the Oscar Wilde's sound
like a tinkling cymbal. His wisdom resembles Solomon's, being

unoriginal; Job-like his fortitude in adversity or grief; and if you suppose that you can twist him round your little finger, try to sell him something . . . and afterwards discover what kind of a pup you have bought. Even amid the fun of the fair and the excitement of the pony auction—even when the Indian fortune-teller has foretold good luck—still the farmer indicts the Government and proscribes the weather. But inwardly he disbelieves his own despair, as V. Sackville-West knew when she called him

> The husbandman who sets his field
> And knows his reckoned crop will come to birth
> Varying but little in its yield
> After the necessary months ensealed
> Within the good the generative earth. . . .

Like everyone else, the farmers and their men are not sages who alone hold the key to a useful and happy life. Many of them remain unaware of their limitations. They do not care for ballet, and have never heard of Pinter. Yet they speak so plainly that only a truthful man will report their speech. When, for example, the Ministry has sent them an especially stupid letter, the farmers exclaim: "There's times I do think I'll pack it in and take a factory job and then draw the dole while a shop steward gets me another quid a week so's I can buy a coloured television." And when their teenage son oversteps the trend, they shout: "Get that bloody hair cut or I'll tan 'ee twice round the sheep-dip."

At Bampton Fair you meet the men who give you hope when the headlines have drained the last drop of it; men who stand up while the National Anthem is played, and are proud to doff their cap when the parson passes by; men who favour England, and cannot understand why England favours so much that is alien; men who see no valid reason why they should drive on the French-hand side of the road, nor pay for their beer in pernickety points of a devalued florin. And when you remind such a farmer that the English must either export or die, he will say to you: "Die? My God, man, what makes 'ee think they'm still alive?"

11

Down in the Forest

The first days of November witness the climax of autumn colouring. Frost and gales will have thinned the leaves, but the survivors outshine the fallen. Seen from a distance, beeches create a late bronze age, and cherry trees resemble pink-coated foxhunters. The effect is so dazzling that you tend not to enter a wood at all, but remain outside, admiring the gorgeous façade. When you do enter, you discover that woods are the deepest part of any landscape. Mountains may appear more solitary, but having climbed them you overlook much company. A wood offers no such prospect. Even the way through it is a path, or at best a track, and the silence seems so profound that when you step on a twig the echo rebounds like the crack of a pistol. Disraeli—who loved his beechwoods at Hughenden—once said: "A forest is like an ocean, monotonous only to the ignorant."

The leafy carpet is not merely ornamental. Many a man has navigated a starless night by listening to the swish of his footsteps. When the sound slackened, he knew that he had strayed from the hollow path; when it grew too loud, he knew that he had strayed again, into a deeper hollow by the way. It is easy to lose yourself in a dark wood at night, and not very difficult to lose your patience also, which is halfway to losing your nerve.

A man may hold the title-deeds of a wood, and yet remain a stranger to its inhabitants. When he walks down the glade, a jay shrieks, a squirrel squawks, a pigeon takes off, cumbrous as a Flying Fortress overladen with looted grain. Each in its own language is saying: "Watch out. Here comes a stranger." The stranger himself cannot always identify the natives by their foot-steps. A leaf stirs, ten yards away, and he waits for the fieldmouse to appear. But it never does appear, because the leaf was stirred by a breeze. On the edge of the wood, where it adjoins a meadow, hares sound like a blackbird that has hopped in. Sometimes the rustling becomes so loud that a fox seems imminent; yet it was only a beetle which had undermined a fallen bough. Despite the sense of being enclosed, a wood in deep country emphasises its own surroundings, so that the eye reads the wind, vigilant as Walt Whitman:

> I inhale great draughts of space,
> The east and the west are mine,
> And the north and the south are mine.

Our trees do not grow so high as they used. It is rare to find one at 1,800 feet, though their roots have been unearthed on the summit of Cross Fell in Cumberland, not far short of 3,000 feet. In Scotland they have been found above 3,000 feet. Botanists believe that felling, not climate, caused our mountains to go thin on top. Thus, in 1608 the New Forest contained 123,927 trees that were registered as suitable for ship-building; less than a century later the number had dwindled to 12,000. At about the same time, when the Duke of Gordon felled the Forest of Badenoch, thousands of trees were floated down the River Spey to the London Timber Company's saw-mills at Garmouth. Philip of Spain understood the worth of our trees when he ordered his Armada to raze the Forest of Dean, a source so valuable that Drake and Raleigh reconnoitred it, seeking timber for their ships. Another who valued our trees was Vice-Admiral Collingwood, to whom fell the honour of leading the Fleet into action at Trafalgar. Admiral Collingwood wrote: "What I am most anxious about is the plantation of oaks in the country. We shall never cease to be a great people while we have ships, which we cannot have without timber. . . . I plant an oak wherever I have place for it." At the Admiral's former estate, near Hethpool in Northumberland, a plantation is known as the Collingwood Oaks.

When Gerard Manley Hopkins mourned the felling of his Binsey aspens, he was pouring old wine into new bottles. More than a thousand years ago St Columba anathematised any who should raze his earthly paradise:

My Derry! my Derry! my little oak-grove,
My dwelling, my home, my own little cell,
May God the Eternal in Heaven above
Send death to thy foes, and defend thee well.

Despite the axe, there are some famous trees alive in Britain.
The oldest (they say) is a yew tree at Fortingall in Perthshire.
When I last saw it, the postman said to me: "Yon was a thousand
years old on the first Christmas Day." A forester was more
explicit; the tree, he estimated, was at least three thousand years

old; as long ago as 1772 its circumference exceeded fifty-six feet.
Another Scottish veteran—in Jedburgh Forest—is thought to
have been planted before the Norman Conquest: certainly it has
received much arboreal dentistry, and the lowermost boughs are
supported by pit props. During the reign of George II an artist
painted a water colour of Bampton church in Devon, showing
two yews near the porch. The trees are still there—encircled by a
stone seat—and they, too, have had their caries removed. At

Tunstead, the Derbyshire birthplace of James Brindley, is a tree called Brindley's Ash, though it seems more likely to be a successor thereof. However, an ash really did start to grow through the floor of Brindley's cottage, and in the end the cottage was demolished in order to preserve its non-paying guest. Near the source of the Thames, in the churchyard at Kemble, there is—or recently was—a yew with another tree growing inside it. Thirty years ago the ferryman at Bablockhythe referred to a riverside coppice as "Th'old umbrella."

A wood is indeed a fine place from which to savour the rain without being soaked by it. Even the barest branches offer some shelter. Holly leaves become green eyes perpetually shedding thankful tears. Twigs juggle an armful of mercurial droplets that disappear one by one over the brink of their own rainbow. And when at last you return home, and are in bed, falling asleep, your thoughts (if they are quiet) will be lulled by the gale that seems to bring the sea ashore.

The Protestants

They always build the Guy Fawkes bonfire on the same spot, at the same height, and so nearly the same size that I sometimes wonder whether they use the same twigs, bracken, and branches.

The spot, by the way, is on a hill; and I say 'spot' because that seems the most accurate description of a community too small even to be called a hamlet. I can tell you exactly how small: one farmhouse, two farm cottages, five other buildings, and a pillar box lashed to a tree stump (I once caught my hand in it, trying to post a tin of tobacco).

Now there are some seasonal events whose opening I always attend—the first snowdrop, the first primrose, the first cuckoo— but I confess that I have yet to attend the laying of the bonfire's foundation. At some time, obviously, an October's child or its father drags the first branches to the site, but I am never there to see it. Whenever I do pass by, the pyre is already three feet on its way to reaching a dozen. Its birth, in short, is as elusive as a mushroom's.

The *auto-da-fé* occurs in a setting as pleasant as any in England, at a clearing among woods by the summit of a steeply winding lane. On all sides, no matter where nor how far you look, other hills rise up, vivid with autumnal leaves. It is a quiet place, too, because the nearest very main road lies six miles to the south, and although the valley road does carry traffic, it is seldom of the lorry sort. In fact, we have retained a high standard of living. The bonfire itself is preceded by a fireproof preview for those whom I call the tot-Prots or, in less theological language, the under-fives. Theirs is a pretty ceremony, but less colourful than the other because it consists solely of sparklers. Having registered their approval of Parliament, and their disapproval of Popery, these Youngest Christians are led away to tea. A non-religious interlude follows, lasting as a rule for about two hours. Then, at seven o'clock or thereabouts, my dog perks up from his fireside rug, growling. I, of course, being only *homo sapiens*, have to see what he has heard. So I draw the curtains; and, sure enough, a rocket is falling below the opposite hill. Twenty minutes later, dog and I reach the scene, having heard and watched much of it while we hurried down the steep lane, and then slowed up the other one. There we join an intimate gathering, seldom above twenty people, sometimes only a dozen; all local; and perhaps one-in-five of them a churchgoer.

The celebrations are ecumenical. Ochred by firelight to look like Hardy's reddleman, a High Anglican ignites his Roman Candle while a visiting Papist prepares to spin his Canterbury Wheel. A Wesleyan and an atheist stand by, ready to fire a 'jumping cracker'. For miles around, every farm dog makes the welkin bark, and during a lull you may sometimes hear a frightened filly thudding through her pitch-black meadow in the valley. At a time when religion has been diagnosed as dead, it is curious to find so many and such zealous Protestants giving thanks that, after all, Guy Fawkes did not breach parliamentary privilege. Concerning Fawkes himself, however, I find a degree of scepticism amounting to agnosticism. Crowned by Mum's old hat, his effigies scarcely do justice to one who was heir to a property in Yorkshire, and had moreover served as sapper officer with the Spanish army (which caused him to be co-opted as the plot's detonator). Nor does the average Protestant know that the plotters had several aims: to kidnap the Duke of York, for instance, and proclaim him as a Roman Catholic king; to seize the infant Princess, lest the Duke escaped, or decided that

London was not worth a Mass; and to raise a rebellion through-out the land. So far from being caught by chance at the last moment, Fawkes had been watched for several days; and within forty-eight hours of his arrest the Privy Council actually printed the names of the chief plotters, together with the punishment awaiting all "who shall in any wise either receive, abette, cherish, entertaine, or adhere unto them . . .". That stern proclamation carried a footnote, as though to uplift from obscurity a name which would otherwise have become less than a name: "Im-printed at London by Edward Barker. Printer to the King's most Excellent majestie, Anno Dom, 1605."

You may recall the doggerel with which Protestant urchins solicited our 'copper' long ago:

> Please to remember
> The Fifth of November
> The Gunpowder, Treason, and Plot.

It is unlikely that the urchins had ever heard their jingle's second stanza:

> I see no reason
> Why the Gunpowder Treason
> Should ever be forgot.

Thomas Carlyle approved such long hindsight: "The three great elements of modern civilization," he declared, "are gunpowder, printing, and the Protestant religion." But Queen Victoria dis-agreed. Urged by her German Consort to dish the Tories, she deleted from the Prayer Book several forms of thanksgiving: one for the escape of Charles II into Boscobel Oak; another, for the escape of Parliament out of its own cellars. Admittedly the Treason thanksgiving gave rather more punches than it pulled, by arrainging Roman Catholics as "bloody Papists" and "devilish enemies".

Those "old unhappy far-off things, and battles long ago" have ceased to scar the British countryside, though their echoes con-tinue to scare some of its inhabitants. It is true to say that none of Her Majesty's subjects—not even the devoted Ulstermen—are more loyal than the average Roman Catholic. It is also true to say that Mammon continues to serve God so well that, on 5th November, the night sky over England glows more lurid than ever it was during the blitz. I remember driving to Cornwall on Guy Fawkes night, not many years ago. As I crossed Bodmin Moor it seemed as though I were in Tudor Cornwall whereon the beacons blazed against an approaching Armada; and when I halted to drink coffee, even there, within sight of the sea, I heard dogs barking, and birds squawking, and somewhere the hooves of a horse.

New Lamps for Old

I first got wind of the change when two men with spades appeared on a field in the valley. So I went to investigate.

"Drains for the farm?" I asked.

"No," they replied. "Electricity for the cottage."

Now unless you happen to live in deep country you will be surprised that any cottage should lack electricity. When an Exmoor housewife was asked why she still used her grandmother's oil lamps and kitchen range, she replied: "They wanted to charge two thousand pounds for putting it in. So I said to my husband . . . we'm not paying two thousand just so's they can send electricity bills."

But to return to the cottage: it was of brick and flint, halfway down a steep hill, two miles from the village. Thirty years ago I could have bought it for ninety pounds. Today it would fetch forty times that sum, partly because it has been modernised. I have watched that modernisation over the years. First came a 'proper lavatory' followed by a bathroom. Then the scullery was transformed into a deep-sink kitchen. After that, stone steps replaced a mud-path from the lane. Finally, two English windows became a French one. All the innovations seemed agreeable. They made life pleasanter and not less homely. Moreover the log fires continued, and with them the oil lamps and candles. And I supposed they always would continue, until, as I say, the spademen appeared, and the cottage soon afterwards sprouted a television aerial.

The owners had vowed that they never would discard their oil lamps, but in the end they did. I cannot blame them, though I do share the regret which they still acknowledge. In one sense, of course, very little has changed; in another sense everything seems different. When I enter the cottage I am no longer greeted by shadowy softness. Instead, I blink at a fluorescent glare. Gone are the nights when I could say with Walter de la Mare:

> The oil in wild Aladdin's lamp
> A witching radiance shed.

Let us be quite clear about this. I am not inviting every country housewife to cook dinner on a smoky range nor to light a candle whenever she goes to see whether the children are asleep. I am simply saying that oil lamps and candles are unique and therefore inimitable. More than any other feature, their disappearance changes the character of a house, and of a village, too, especially when it is inhabited by people who leave an electric light blazing at their front door. Oil lamps blend with every rural scene. In my own porch a hurricane lamp burns throughout the night; partly to deter villains, partly to identify visitors, and partly to cheer any traveller through the hills.

So far from praising times past, my own immediate reaction is to say: "Modern stoves and lighting are a necessity. Anyone who chooses to do without them is a crank." Yet second thoughts recall some words by a man who knew more than most people about the deepest needs of human nature: "I have done without electricity," wrote Jung, "and tend the fireplace and stove myself. Evenings, I light the old lamps. There is no running water, and I pump the water from the well. I chop the wood and cook the food. These simple acts make man simple; and how hard it is to be simple."

As a child I grew up by candle-light, and can still remember the shadows—sometimes menacing, sometimes companionable—that climbed with me when I creaked upstairs to bed at the top of a rambling country house. Even now I often read myself to sleep by candle-light. Electricity, after all, makes a bedroom seem glazed and predictable, like noon in the tropics. No flickering shadows add edge to a ghostly tale; no sudden draught rings down a curtain more dramatic than the playwright's. A good candle gives an adequate light, and our ancestors' eyesight may have been sharpened by it. Said Carlyle: "How inferior, for seeing with, is your brightest train of fireworks, to the humblest farthing candle." And the candle returns the compliment, as Isaac Bicker-staff knew when he remarked of a not-so-youngster: "By candle-light nobody would have taken you for above five-and-twenty."

I once spoke with an Oxfordshire villager who remembered the years when the firm of Haynes supplied several tons of rush-lights annually to Oxford and Cambridge. Gilbert White, some-time Vice-Provost of Oriel, conducted an experiment which showed that a single reed gave "a good clear light" for fifty-seven minutes. Lighting in those days cost a cottager one farthing for twelve hours. Some cottagers still make rushlights for use on landings and beside the bed. I saw some at John o' Groat's in 1967. Having been spliced, the reeds are dipped in boiling fat . . . six pounds of fat to one of reeds. How precious the light was in those old times, not solely for its cash value. William Tyndale's only surviving letter was written from a dungeon in Brussels, shortly before they strangled him for daring to translate the Bible into English; the letter ended by asking "permission to have a candle in the evening; for it is wearisome to sit alone in the dark".

When you come to think of it, many of the world's crises occurred or were resolved by candle-light. By such light Nelson wrote his orders to the Fleet on the eve of Trafalgar: "If the Enemy are standing to the Southward . . . burn two blue lights together, every hour. . . ." It was by candle-light, surely, that Shakespeare quilled "the way to dusty death . . . out, out, brief candle". And surely by candle-light Beethoven scratched the score of his C sharp minor quartet.

But all that was long ago. Now we press a switch, with effects that can be both charming and troublefree. The days are past when Everyman so feared the night that he anticipated its death, like Robert Herrick's Bell-man:

> Past one aclock, and almost two,
> My Masters all, Good day to you.

Nevertheless, before you do dismiss candles and lamps as wholly out-dated, ask yourself whether you have never entered a farm-house at night, wishing devoutly that you too might work in the open air, and afterwards relax by lamplight.

The Last of England

"When you have lost your inns, you will have lost the last of England." Hilaire Belloc spoke the truth, and then capped it with a drinking song:

> My jolly fat host with your face all a-grin,
> Come, open the door to us, come let us in.
> A score of stout fellows who think it no sin
> If they toast till they're hoarse, and they drink
> till they spin. . . .

There are several pubs in the village—well-conducted, well-appointed, well-patronised—but they are not what you and I mean by an old country pub. They have high-heeled stools, for one thing; and electric lights got-up to resemble candles. Such places please the new kind of villager, but the old breed prefers the old pub, which, when I first knew it, was lit by oil lamps and a log fire. Even today the electric light bulb is shadeless. There are, moreover, no price-distinctions between Lounge and Public. You simply walk in, and there you are, in a snug room with beech logs casting aromatic shadows on walls whose pin-ups announce *For Sale By Auction. 5 Tons Hay, 2 Tractors, Farm Implements, etc.* The pub has no chromium stools padded bright red like a baboon's behind. Customers sit on a deal bench at a scrubbed table, playing dominoes. Edmund Blunden might have looked in, to feel the pulse of rural England:

> Round all its nooks and corners goes
> The evening talk at this old inn;
> The darkening room by use well knows
> Each thread of life that these up-spin.

Mind you, the pub moves with the times. As recently as 1953 the portrait of King George V was replaced by a picture of the landlord's battalion advancing on Mons. The spittoons went at about the same time, and now offer drinks-on-the-house to all dogs. Occasionally the place is patronised by the steadier element among the under-forties. Indeed, I have seen motor-cycles parked outside, and through the window somebody's long curls tickling the same body's short beard (but now I come to think of it, I have never seen a woman at the pub). Nevertheless, symptoms of progress keep pace with events. Men whose grandfathers raised six children on thirty shillings a week, now recount their own expensive misadventures in London: "Oi reckon thart ol' restont's a ruddy swizzle, oi do. Oi took the ol' woman there last Sartdee, and we paid a ruddy quid. Oi said to her when we got bark, 'Girl,' oi said, 'we'd ha' done better down the Cosy Caif. They can print the name in French,' oi said, 'but it's still fish-and-chips'."

Nowadays we all drink at village inns, which is one reason why so few of them remain. A true village inn is a place where the under-a-thousand-a-year men may meet—and drink and be merry —without feeling constrained by the camouflaged condescension of people who have a slightly different accent and a very different income. It is a place where settled men—and boys before the Dance—can discuss corn and the Colonel's new mare without needing to turn a deafened ear on a too-long-playing-juke-box. Above all, it is a place where as many things as possible remain as nearly the same as they always have been. In short, it is a place which Hilaire Belloc had in mind when he declared: "From the towns all Inns have been driven . . . from the villages most. . . ."

And what a long lineage lay behind them. When the Normans arrived—a wine-drinking crew—they found in Britain the *eala-hus* or ale-house. Chaucer's great journey began from an inn:

> —in Southwerk at the Tabard as I lay
> Redy to wenden on my pilgrimage
> To Caunterbury. . . .

If Venus arose from the water, then Falstaff, surely, was conceived in Sack or Spanish wine, and may have been born therein while Bardolph jostled Shakespeare's quill: "O monstrous! but one half-pennyworth of bread to this intolerable deal of sack!" Dickens—that roving reporter—littered his landscape with country taverns. Edward Thomas savoured the bliss that comes after a good meal and before a warm bed at a country inn:

> No traveller has rest more blest
> Than this moment. . . .

Of the few remaining country inns, all must adapt themselves to safety-first laws that were long overdue. Drunken driving,

N

however, is not likely to be indulged by customers at our village inn, most of whom live within ten minutes' walk of it, and some next door, or across the street. On very special occasions—a victory by the darts team at home, or the sexton's retirement—one or two of the celebrants may be found awake in the gutter, but never asleep at the wheel.

Meanwhile, although the old order changeth, it has not yet been demolished, for there are still some inns that burn oil lamps; others, that hold only a beer licence; a few, so remote that

their landlords rely on a smallholding. I know one Devonshire inn whose bar is the living room and very nearly the only room. In Herefordshire there is an inn where you can pay your bill by helping to make the publican's half-acre of hay. Hidden among the moors of County Durham, tap rooms echo to country talk that will baffle any man south of Yorkshire. Off the holiday track in Cornwall, or deep in the Leicestershire coverts . . . there, on a November night, are pubs where two or three foregather in much the same manner as Piers Plowman and his pals when they supped ale on the Malvern Hills eight hundred years ago; twentieth-century men, booted and gaitered and so timelessly coated that you cannot tell whether they bring news of the Armada, or are up-to-date and have come to announce the relief of Mafeking.

This state of country affairs may be desirable, or it may be undesirable, according as you define good and evil. But one fact remains beyond dispute: the true village inn survives because those who do not pertain to it do not pretend to it. Though I sometimes glance through the window, I have never entered the 'Wheatsheaf'.

Halcyon Days

Anchored safely up-stream at her winter berth, *Noah's Ark* seemed snugly secure, hemmed-in by hills that hid the sea. I therefore looked forward to a quiet night while the rich men's summer yachts, moored near the harbour, tugged at their wave-swept chain.

My hopes were ill-founded. Coming on deck to check the anchor, I noticed that the wind had veered and was now blowing force eight from the south-east, the one quarter which regards the creek as a wind-tunnel, and yachts as toys to be dragged with their moorings. I could truthfully say with John Donne:

> Sooner than you read this line, did the gale,
> Like shot, not fear'd till felt, our sailes assaille;
> And what at first was call'd a gust, the same
> Hath now a storme's, anon a tempest's, name.

All night I was awake, with both feet wedged against the locker seat, sometimes holding a saucepan of cocoa onto the oil stove. Outside, the wind howled; waves jabbed unending uppercuts that jerked the bows out of the water; *Noah's Ark* endured all the rigours of a seaway, but without any of the verve of moving forward. At about six in the morning I fell asleep where I sat.

Next thing I remember, I was aroused by a sound, or rather by an absence of sound . . . and of motion, too. Opening my eyes, I blinked at the blue glare streaming through the portlights. Fifty yards away, on shore, a robin trilled. Sheep in the hills grazed safely. And a peckish tapping for'ard announced that the swans were reminding me that I was late for their breakfast. I entered the cock-pit, staring in amazement because—not six feet away—a millionaire's cruiser loomed above me. Several moments passed, before I understood that she had dragged her moorings for two-thirds of a mile. And what was that, three hundred yards astern?— *Clarissa*, a two-ton yacht, high-and-half-filled on the bank, with the branch of a tree bent around her samson post. Port and star-board a cargo of driftwood, seaweed, and other flotsam littered the shore. Yet the water was as calm as a June night, and over the hill-top the sun stood like a golden sovereign.

I turned first to the stores, ruefully re-arranging the night's disorder, extracting sugar from marmalade, and sea boots from bilge water. That done, the swans and I made a hearty breakfast; after which, I lit a pipe, and then leaned against the wheel, savouring the solitude. At about this hour, I thought, countless millions are motoring, cycling, straphanging, and generally yawning their way from one kind of noise to another. Not for an instant throughout the day will they be truly alone, com-municating with themselves. Even their lavatories are loud with Mammon's witless gabble. Yet here am I, alone upon salt water; in one sense as marooned as though I were on a raft in mid-Atlantic; in another sense, so close to my fellowkind that I can see smoke twining from a distant cottage. If a man is very rich, or content to remain rather poor, the best of those two worlds will meet him by arrangement.

Even in these automatic days a seaman lives his life apart; and in small boats especially that life differs from a landsman's. The difference itself is something more than a litany of seafaring terms—'deck' instead of 'floor', 'alongside' instead of 'against', 'scuttle' instead of 'window'. It is something more than pilotage and the ability to gauge your ship's ability. It is basically a domestic difference. In the first place, you must be tidy, because if you are not, life soon becomes uncomfortable, then unbearable, and ultimately hazardous (it is no use chucking the anchor into a tangle of chain). Above all, you must be punctual because, like time itself, the tide does not wait upon your convenience. If you arrive too early, a rock will bar the fairway; if too late, mud will have replaced the fairway. If moreover your ship is as old and as primitive as mine was, you must make-do with the minimum of gadgets. Only innate skill, and years of erring trial, can teach you to fend for yourself against the sea, that enigmatic neutral which may without warning become either your ally or your executioner.

After breakfast I steered downstream, not along the channel, but in and out of it whenever a plank, or a lobster pot, or a crate of merchandise loomed up like a mine. Four times I sighted a craft that had dragged her moorings and was being retrieved by boatmen. I went alongside the jetty, tied-up, and passed a companionable hour among old seamen with long memories: "Must have been nineteen-o-five or thereabouts. It blew all day and then it blew all night. The ferry didn't put-out. Lord What's-his-name's yacht were found topside-down on the Manacles. And old Granny Trewin had her roof tore away. Not that I'm grumbling, mind. I've just took a fiver off the doctor for getting his cruiser back. I told 'en teatime yesterday, her wouldn't ride it out. But no, he wasn't going to bother. Suits me, though. Couple more nights like that and I'll be evading super-tax."

Back at her secluded berth, *Noah's Ark* basks in the light of a St Martin's summer so mild that I take my lunch in the cock-pit, whence I pay-out the praam, speckled with bread crumbs for a robin that has learned to hop on board for his dinner. In every sense a sea-dog, my passenger strolls along the narrow combing, jumps into the returning praam, and sits there, bolt upright in the stern, a captain with his own corner of the quarter-deck. Far out to sea a tanker's siren mimics the voice of destiny, partly a challenge, partly a warning, partly an invitation. And when the last gruff boom has died away, a sheep bleats, a dog barks, and the boatman clip-clops home to dinner, stooping slightly while he flicks one oar with manner-born wrist. Having come within hailing distance, he addresses the sky: "Looks like the wind's backed round where 'en belongs. We'm in for a fine spell." Then he addresses *Noah's Ark*: "Going to watch the darts match to-night?"

"Maybe," I reply; adding to myself, "unless I'm reading an old poet, or a new economist, or just watching the stars while they walk on the water."

News from the Mountains

The first snowflake fell without a sound; but the second, alighting on the hurricane lamp, uttered a sigh as it expired. By the time I reached the shippon the night had changed from black to white. Inside, I hooked the lamp to a rafter, and then stood still, looking and listening. Although the door was shut, a crystal mat seeped through a crevice underneath. Overhead, the ceiling lurched with the shadows of a hunchback giant—my own shoulders whenever I moved. The wind howled like a wolf. Now and again a sudden gust lifted wisps of straw, as though urging them to join the carnival outside. Hearing it, the two cows—Lavender and Lilac—looked round, clinking their chains with a music thin as the wren's song.

"Coom up!"

Cows have a sideways kick when they choose; and being half a guest, I must have seemed to them wholly a stranger. This was sheep country, but the farmer himself, who lived beyond a dairy round, had a growing family, so he kept two cows which were milked by hand. I glanced at my own hands. Although they were by no means city-soft, it was many years since they had learned to milk a cow. As I sat astride the stool, I recalled that distant initiation, in a shippon much the same as this, though away in the New Forest of Hampshire, not among the mountains of Wales. However, I took comfort from something that Dai the shepherd had said: "Mr Peel, bach, you have missed the boat. It is a farmer you should have been, not a poet." But with the next breath he recanted, remembering—as every Welshman does remember—the poets of his own people: "And yet, you know, Dafydd ap Gwilym was a great man. You have read his poem to the lark, I shouldn't wonder. A very fine poem that. It begins . . . but there, I am forgetting . . . it was you who told me how it does begin:

> Up the familiar skies ascend,
> And leave the level fallow land;
> God has given you gifts enough
> Before his face in worship to go."

I remembered my thumbed copy of Dr Fream's *Elements of*

Agriculture, 1918, which stated: "There is no farm operation that requires more skill than milking, when effectively carried out. The milker should always speak to the cow when approaching, taking the stool in the left hand and the milk-pail in the right." No wonder the *Elements* became the textbook for the Active Service Army Schools.

"Coom up, then."

Despite a propitiating pat, Lavender remained ominously neutral. "She that is not with us," I feared, "must be agin." But I was unjust. Once my fingers had re-learned past lessons, Lavender lived up to her lovely name. Within a few moments I forgot the snow, and became engrossed in the rhythmic music . . . a thumping storm, the staccato clink, jaws champing, somewhere the sheep bleating, and, over all, the whine of milk upon metal. How many poets, I wondered, had set this scene to song; and how few of them had ever practised it. Yet Robert Frost knew what he was writing about when he cited his own sick cow:

> She bellows on a knoll against the sky.
> Her udders shrivel and the milk runs dry.

And Edward Jenner knew, when he wrote *Berkeley Fair*:

> The rosy milkmaid grabs her pail. . . .

Nor was that a poetical cliché, for out of his milking came cowpox and the vaccine which saved innumerable lives.

When you milk by hand, the stripping or final yield is of the utmost importance. If you know the cow, you know also when that moment approaches. The knowledge is intuitive and at the same time sensory because you gauge it via the level in the bucket —and *that* you gauge without looking, by the crescendo. If you had told Vergil, or even Thomas Hardy, that the cow would one day be milked by machine, they would have tapped their forehead. And if you had said that work itself seemed likely to become a twice-weekly interlude between the business of doing nothing in particular, they would have turned away as from a madman. I would have done the same myself, that night when a Hampshire farmer—having confronted me with a cow, a bucket, a stool—remarked: "The best way to learn is to learn. I'll be back in ten minutes."

Now all is changed. Instead of sharing timeless things with

those who delight in them, a chronicler of the countryside finds that he is partly an antiquarian and partly a pioneer, footsore from limping after the latest innovation. Pausing to uncrick my spine, I wondered whether a counter-revolution would set in, with men growing rich by renting Milka-Cow to people who had grown weary of trips to the moon. But second thoughts revised their first version, and a glance at the shippon confirmed them, for this was a small farm in a remote place, lit by oil lamps and candles; so intent on minding its own business that a weekly visit to the market town seemed always a spree, and became sometimes an adventure (tonight not even the tractor could plough through its own snowbound ruts).

Very carefully I removed the bucket, remembering the night when my first pailful was kicked across the concrete, to the tune of some of the loudest oaths that ever rent the New Forest . . . not my oaths . . . they came from the farmer, who had returned in tigm to see his pupil on the ground, and his milk in the conduit. Havine set the yield safely against a wall, I turned to Lilac, and found her as amenable as Lavender. At the end of it all, I glanced at the crystal mat under the door, and saw it had risen several inches. The sight reminded me that I was cold. My back ached, and my fingers were swollen, but I had recaptured an ancient skill, in a setting not greatly different from its mediaeval ancestor.

Unhooking the lantern, I took a last glance around. Lavender and Lilac were at ease, nuzzling supper from a wooden rack. Suddenly the old words came to me, a little in advance of their season: "and she wrapped him in swaddling clothes and laid him in a manger . . .".

I 2

Winterscape

A film of ice covered the window when I awoke, hovering above my head like a halo. Then the cold air slipped down to my nose, and would have wrapped itself into a necklace had I not tugged the blanket over my mouth. Ten minutes later, standing by the opaque window, I heard my teeth chattering to the tune of Robert Herrick:

> I freeze, I freeze, and in me dwells
> Nothing but snow, and icicles.

There seemed every reason to remain by the fire, and none at all to venture beyond it . . . until I opened the front door, and saw the wizardry of frost. The lawn sparkled like the base of a wedding cake. Clods of earth, hard now as granite, resembled a diamond-digger's dream, glinting under the brilliant sky. Withered cow parsley mimed a powdered cactus. Yesterday's raindrops were stalactites on every twig. Comical to watch, one robin landed on a frozen puddle, and then overshot the runway. Falling to the ground, a beech leaf bounced instead of bending; when touched, it snapped in half, brittle as burned toast. You would suppose that whiteness never could improvise on the unvarying theme of its own monotone, yet it does, for a hoar frost resembles an etching, whereas deep snow falls as it were on a canvas, so that each creates a paradox because the snow cannot be suggested (it must be explained in detail), and the frost cannot be explained (it needs a Japanese line or two). Blizzards seem often baroque, especially when a wind has piled-on the ornamentation;

frost wears always a Benedictine bareness. Faced by the *fait-accompli*, I followed Burns's advice, turning resignation into exultation:

> Blow, blow, ye winds, with heavier gust!
> And freeze, thou bitter-biting frost!
> Descend, ye chilly smothering snows!

In the village street everyone walked warily; only the veterans appeared at ease, pursuing the even tempo of their ways. The milk van, I noticed, had come to grief, and was being extracted from the doctor's garden. Anticipating snow, the Royal Mail clinked like a convict in chains, spitting specks of grit from its wheels. And everywhere the cottagers compared notes: "My chilblains blaze redder than a crop o' tomatoes." . . . " 'Call this coal?' I said. " 'Tis the best fire-extinguisher I've ever bought'." . . . "They'm that mean they won't never light the fire till they'm too cold to strike a match." . . . "So she come across after breakfast and says, 'Even the bloody fridge is froze.' "

While children scan the sky, seeking a snow cloud, persons of riper years look back upon their own callow season, trying to recall a comparably cold spell, even as Parson Woodforde recalled the Norfolk winter of 1785: "The frost," he reported, "froze the Chamber Pots under the Beds." Villagers become conscious of draughts from open doors, especially in shops, where each new customer is disapproved by his shivering predecessors; but the Post Office engineers sit snugly at their brazier, sipping tea. Down in the valley, they say, trains are late because points are frozen; and the hardware shop ran out of paraffin last night. Foxes walk abroad at noon, toppling the dustbin lids (during the winter of 1963 they roamed the main street of East Grinstead). Somewhere —it always happens in bitter cold—the oldest inhabitant succumbs at last, and the news is slow to get around because the lanes, too, are tardy: "Crouched over her grate she was, poor old soul. Just died o' the cold." It is the same among the birds: you see them in the lane, or frozen to their perch, embalmed while they slept. The survivors haunt the water-butt, bewildered by its solidarity.

There is so little traffic that you suddenly remember what England was like in the quiet old days; and when at last a car does approach, you stand still, waiting for it not to skid. Out in the fields, if you slip on a furrow, you risk breaking an ankle or grazing the skin. If you strike the furrow with your stick, the ferrule emits sparks; yet the thaw when it comes will crumble those impenetrable cliffs into a friable tilth. Away on the hills a horn halloos, and presently the beaglers' green coats cross the skyline; hounds, you fancy, are indulging some unofficial sport with rabbits that have broken cover in search of food.

In the woods, where nothing has thawed, the leaves underfoot rustle like tissue paper, so that every bird betrays its wandering whereabouts, and even the mice sound loud. If by mischance a hibernating creature awakes today, without at once dropping off to sleep again, it will surely perish. Perhaps the cold has spliced an oak, which startled you because there really was an explosion and afterwards the anguished crunch of the falling tree. All stars appear to dance—there is no other word for it—literally jumping up and down, or jigging from side to side, playing strange tricks on the retina. The woodshed seems to have been sprinkled with sugar—each granule a gem—and if you touch it, the frost rasps a bare finger. When the moon emerges from a cloud, the fields are flooded white as snow. The air is so taut that you hear a dog rattling his chain at the hilltop farm a mile away. And the owl quavers, like an old man on a draughty platform. In summer you would have said: "There's not a breath of wind anywhere." Now you say: "The air's like a knife."

At mid-day, when several clouds appear, it looks as though the cold has passed its zenith, and will abate. Certainly the barbed wire begins to drip, and the fringe of puddles show a kind of surf. But toward teatime the clouds disperse; a blood-orange sun sinks into its own furnace; and with nightfall a new wave of frost arrives, keener than ever.

Long after the light has failed, a pool beyond the village echoes to the sibilance of Wordsworth's boyhood lake:

> All shod with steel,
> We hissed along the polished ice . . .
> The leafless tree and every icy crag
> Tinkled like iron. . . .

Through uncurtained windows a glowing beech log writes Welcome on the mat of your imagination, all the more cordial because, when you reach the porch, with one gloved hand on the latch, you overhear the sound of things freezing without sound, and the bark of a famished vixen.

An Expedition to the Shops

Shopping is easy for people whose needs are as modest as their income. The other day, for instance, I shouldered a knapsack, whistled the dog, and walked four miles to buy some Christmas presents at the nearest village. The way thither is steep and in places so narrow that, on the rare occasion when a car does appear, you must either flatten yourself against the bank or risk having your toes punctured. Only half-a-dozen cottages and farms are passed *en route*, but a river tumbles alongside, singing treble to precipitous woods above. In late autumn a deer will sometimes roar a warning to any wanton that would take-over his herd of hinds.

You approach the village by loping down a steep lane, yet the place itself stands seven hundred feet above the sea and almost within sight of it. Moreover, the village can seem very elusive, being divided into two parts, of which the higher—called Church Town—is a windswept hamlet overlooking the shopping centre far below. Misled by the word 'Town' on a signpost, the stranger (if he ever does pass that way) grinds his car up a hairpin cul-de-sac, and is dismayed to find only a derelict church and a handful of cottages. When at last he does reach the shopping centre, he may still fail to find more than half of it because the other two shops lie some way up another steep lane.

It must be said at once that certain commodities are not on sale in the village, not even during the Christmas rush; mink coats, for example. Nor would you be well-advised to go there in search of caviare or a gold wristwatch. But if you belong among the modest shoppers, you will find more than at first meets the eye, even although the shop windows are not flecked with cotton wool (people who expect to be snowbound feel no inclination to tempt the genuine particle).

I timed my own arrival for late afternoon when the light was failing, and the shop windows shone—all four of them—though none so gaily as the General Stores. There I bought for my great-nephew a gift costing two shillings. His sister—being still at a stage when the tongue can taste but not yet speak—received an item of food similar to the brand which Father Christmas delivered for myself at that age; but the cost of reindeer food and the maintenance of sledges appeared to have risen by six hundred per cent. Even so, you must not dismiss me as a Great-Uncle Scrooge. The children will receive other gifts, bought from two of the other three shops. The Stores, after all, enjoys the best site in town, and it would have been uncharitable not to patronise the tradesmen whose premises were tucked away, up the steep lane.

There is indeed an esoteric or magical atmosphere at Christmas. Consider that homely and least topical of objects, a tin of tobacco. Neither Joseph nor Mary, one supposes, had ever heard of the weed; yet wrap it in red paper, and attach a picture of Santa Claus, and the thing positively reeks of Bethlehem. I say it without offence; rather with gratitude aforethought insofar as I hope to receive a tin myself.

In the second shop I discovered that peace is sometimes divisible, even at Christmas and among people of good will. Thus, one old woman said to the shopman: "Your eyes are sharper than mine. Is this half-a-crown or just another o' they decimals?"

"It's a half-crown," the shopman replied. "In other words, illegal."

"Illegal? Next thing, they'll pass a law against speaking English."

"They've passed one already. What's more, my girl, if they ever do catch you using the word English they'll race you up afore the Relations Board."

"They can race me where they like. We'm Devon down yere, and Devon we'm going to stay. And let other folk stay, too . . . stay where they belong . . . where charity belongs. Then maybe we'll all like ourselves a sight better."

" 'Tis too late for that, my love. The damage is done. Anyhow, yere's your change." Suddenly he snatched the coin back again. "Now 'tis me getting the decimals mixed up. I never could abear the damned things. Even at school I didn't see the point of 'em."

The fourth shop confronted me with a problem because the owner had sold his last sausage. Being (as we say) all right for turkeys, I feared that I must either depart empty-handed or buy a bar of unnecessary chocolate. In the end, however, the dog solved the problem by eating some broken biscuits on the floor.

"We can do better than that, surely," the shopman exclaimed. "Yere, Whiskers, get your teeth into this."

When I offered to pay, the man shook his head: "No, no, I can't charge 'ee for a bit o' biscuit. You what? Well, then, try one o' these pies. I know what's in 'em 'cause I minced it myself."

The village street is so narrow that even six shoppers create a bustle loud as a Kodaly folk dance. I certainly noticed at least one last-minute rush when a breathless woman hurried in: "Have 'ee got any . . . ah, just one packet left, I see. Thank the Lord for that. Ten minutes ago my new daughter-in-law arrived. No telephone nor anything. Well, I mean to say, fancy motoring all the way from Okehampton without even . . . but never mind. Is she what? A mini-skirt? My dear soul, half-an-inch less and she'd be minus a skirt. But never mind. And while I'm yere I'll take a box o' that 'cause next week the price'll go up to keep pace with the cost o' striking. But never mind."

With a full knapsack I turned for home, once or twice glancing back at the festive shops. The stars were out now, and from the highest hill I saw the sea, winking the eye of its lighthouse. An owl hooted from the woods, but the river sang the same song, and at each of the half-dozen cottages the curtained windows smiled like rubies.

It had been a simple shopping expedition, eight miles there and back, costing less than a guinea; but when at last I arrayed my wares on the table, I thought how gay they looked, wrapped in their Santa Claus.

The Music of the Bells

On a frosty Christmas Eve at the beginning of this century the Poet Laureate, Robert Bridges, climbed a hill above his home near Oxford. Entranced by the distant music of church bells, he made a poem, *Noel*:

> A frosty Christmas Eve
> When the stars were shining
> Fared I forth alone

Where westward falls the hill,
And from many a village
In the water'd valley
Distant music reached me
Peals of bells aringing. . . .

The poem may be called a bell-ringer's signature tune, evoking
both the sight and the sound of those

Who are ringing for Christ
In the belfries tonight
With arms uplifted to clutch
The rattling ropes that race
Into the dark above. . . .

It used to be said that the first church bell was introduced by a
fourth-century Bishop of Nola in Campania, but the tradition is
mistaken, having arisen because *nola* and *campana* are late Latin
words for a bell. In 1847 someone invented the word 'campano-
logy' to connote the techniques of bell-ringing and bell-founding.
About five thousand of our churches possess bells, and the ringers
thereof have their own magazine. Bell-ringing, in fact, has
become a pious hobby among all sorts and conditions of men and
women. I know an admiral who pulls his weight every Sunday
and on practice nights also. There is a young lady bell-ringer at
Kirkby Lonsdale in Westmorland, and an old lady bell-ringer (also
deputy sexton) near Great Missenden in Buckinghamshire. I know
an artist bell-ringer at Bideford in Devon; a doctor in Lincolnshire; and a brace of farmers in Cornwall. No great strength is
required; once the bell is under way, even a child can keep time.

The bells themselves are usually maintained by the parochial
church council, and most belfries have their captain, treasurer,
and secretary. The parson is *ex officio* custodian of the bells.
Parson Woodeforde's diary shows that in 1792 he exercised his
right to celebrate a local news item when the squire's lady, well-
loved by the villagers, recovered from a long illness: "Bells
ringing . . . on Account of Mrs Custance coming down stairs for
the first time for the past 5 Months." But news travelled slowly
in those years, and sometimes the ringers were confounded. On
10th November 1805 Wordsworth wrote: "At the breakfast-
table tidings reached us of the death of Lord Nelson and of the
victory at Trafalgar." But at Penrith they knew only of the

triumph: "We were shocked," Wordsworth added, "to hear that the bells had been ringing joyously at Penrith."

The phrase "parish pride" takes on a new note when the belfries join battle

> In steeples far and near,
> A happy noise to hear.

I always like the story of the church whose six bells proudly uttered a challenge: "Who-can-ring-like-we-can?" ... to which a neighbouring belfry replied: "We-can ... we-can ... we-can." The act of bell-ringing has been known to achieve a most remarkable regeneration, even in the oldest Adam. One villager was so given to swearing that not even in church could he curb his gift of tongues. The vicar therefore banished him from the choir to the belfry. After a few weeks the exile reported a dramatic improvement: "Vicar," he declared, "the effect of bell-ringing on my language is nothing short of a bloody miracle."

When a Churchill is buried, the people expect to hear a muffled toll; when a bride is married, they expect to hear the vibrant peal ("Bells," said Thomas Hood, "are Music's laughter"). But to the generality nowadays the music of the bells is simply an echo from the irrevocable past. Sounds more supersonic imperil the fabric of our cathedrals. This was not always so. When the French Revolution banned church bells, the men of La Vendée rose up, and went into their belfries, and rang defiance; and having done so, they sent their *cahiers* or complaints to Paris, demanding to be allowed to summon the faithful, to mourn the departed, and to greet Madame Custance.

Sometimes our church bells have served both God and Mammon, as when Beau Nash persuaded Bath Abbey to salute wealthy visitors with a peal; after which, he presented them with the bill. Such showmanship displeased those who set rank before riches. Tobias Smollett remarked sarcastically: "The Abbey bells began to ring so loud, that we could not hear one another speak; and this peal, as we afterwards learned, was for the honour of Mr Bullock, an eminent Tottenham cowkeeper, who had just arrived to drink the waters for indigestion."

At Christmastime our country belfries extend a different kind of invitation, which many accept after their fashion: "Behold, I stand at the door and knock: if any man hear my voice, and open

o

the door, I will come into him, and will sup with him and he with me." Robert Bridges had long ago accepted that invitation, for he was an accomplished musician who compiled the *Yattendon Hymnal*. When therefore he stood on the Oxfordshire hilltop, listening to the bells, he overheard an even older music, sung by the heavenly host: "Fear not, for, behold I bring you good tidings of great joy, which shall be to all people." Remembering then the story of that first Christmas, the poet found it as fresh as ever, and never before so deep with many meanings:

> The old words came to me
> By the riches of time
> Mellowed and transfigured
> As I stood on the hill
> Hearkening in the aspect
> Of the eternal silence.

A New Day

A country Christmas begins in much the same ways as when it was first celebrated. Coming downstairs, you find the night still enthroned, apparently forever. Lamplight shines as it did at dusk, and although the logs are spent, their ashes will soon kindle dry chips. The dog, hearing familiar footsteps, does not stir from his wise old basket. Clocks tick the same tock as at bedtime. Outside, the same moon is attended by the same stars, and you must look twice before noticing that they have slipped. In the valley a cock crows and is answered. A frozen puddle cracks, curt as a pistol-shot. The rest is silence.

From time to time, while a kettle boils, you peer through the curtains, as though your impatience might arouse the day. But that sky is still dark, the birds asleep. Then a pair of boots clatter the cobbles while a farmhand strikes a match for his hurricane lamp. Presently a bucket rattles from the byre, followed by the whine of milk against metal. Whenever the farmhand opens the byre door, a symphony is heard—of stamping, mooing, clinking—that was old when Bethlehem was young.

After a while the farmhand is joined by Tom, the cart horse.

who has clumped to the yard gate in time for the lump of sugar that had been tucked in the farmhand's pocket by his grand-daughter last night. Usually it is one lump: "But it's Christmas, so I'm going to give him three."

There is only one cow on the farm, and by the time she has been milked, the eastern sky grows pale enough to etch the trees. Seeing them, the farmhand puffs his lamp, lights a pipe, and says "Merry Christmas" to the farmer's wife who has come to put out the cat and the mat (and if one refuses to forsake the other, out they go together, Christmas or no Christmas). The farmhand meanwhile leans against a tractor, admiring the dawn. Such men write no poems, and may speak little enough prose, yet it would be strange indeed were they to ignore a pageant that costs nothing except the effort of waking up, and has therefore not risen in price. It belongs to no party, no creed, no class. Unlike passion, it does not fawn upon youth; unlike wisdom, it needs not wait on age. From time immemorial men have praised the morning.

Now the darkness ebbs away, like water down a drain. One by one night's mysterious shapes become everyday objects: the roof of the barn, the scythe in the hedge, the horse at the gate. Timed by a psychic metabolism, the farmer's wife pulls back the curtains; but the lights are still on, so that the farmhand sees a shop window of seasonable wares—holly, paper-chains, mistle-toe. Another countryman, John Clare, seeing the same sight a century ago, remembered the snows of yesteryear:

> Thou happy day of sound and mirth
> That long with childish memory stays,
> How blest around the cottage hearth
> I met thee in my boyish days.

When at last the kettle whistles its sevenses, the farmhand enters the kitchen, still blowing on his chilblains. Presently the first robin stirs in its roost, uttering five cold notes to announce the fact. Then a sparrow answers, and the dawn chorus begins. Red as a mouth, the sun yawns behind ebony boughs, and its breath is a blush on the sky. Things that were mysterious half an hour ago lose their eerie glamour. The signpost is itself at last, no longer a gallows. The rick, too, is itself, no longer the walls of a castle. Business is as usual. Yet not quite as usual, for when the policeman is sighted, cycling homeward, he is beckoned indoors where mince-pies and teacups are raised in a time-honoured greeting: "Happy Christmas."

"I know who made these pies," says the policeman. "By the way, how's the old man's lumbago?"

"So-so," says the wife. "Though there's times I think 'tis nothing but an acute attack o' breakfast-in-bed."

"Ah, well. He works hard. Besides, it only comes once a year, you know. And the way we'm pushing along, 'tisn't going to come all that often. Strike me, is that the time? I must get cracking."

As the policeman's bicycle crunches up lane, out goes the kitchen light, and day walks in through the window. The housewife looks at her stove, mentally arithmeticking a list that includes washing-up, Church, dishing-up, and then more washing-up.

"Mum!"

She turns, and is greeted by a volley of gunfire lately tugged from a Christmas stocking.

"You're dead, Mum. Merry Christmas!"

Somewhere a radio announces its litany of violence and folly, but is interrupted by a shout from Old Lumbago: "Switch that damned thing off!" The shout is drowned by another rasp of gunfire. Blandly the radio continues "and the strike is estimated to be costing more than five million. . . ."

"Switch it off!"

This time the shout is heard. The litany halts in mid-sentence. The despair of a world whose year is dying is replaced by the hopes of a parish unto whom a new day is born. Some of the parishioners regard the day as special, but in a way which so far passes their understanding that they are content to translate it symbolically. Others abide by Milton's literal interpretation:

This is the Month, and this the happy morn
Wherein the Son of Heav'ns eternal King,
Of wedded Maid, and Virgin Mother born,
Our great redemption from above did bring. . . .

On the Threshold

Bare, bare, bare . . . that is the brusque motto of a new-born year.
Riddled by daylight, the hedges are as bare as a trellis without
roses. The air is bare—so bare that only a non-smoking teetotal
countryman can taste it; and even he will say that it smells like the
tang of cold water. The hills are bare. They are all bare and they
are bare all over. The whole world is bare—bare boughs, bare
fields, and winter wheat bare because half-dressed.

You can see the bareness near, and you can see it afar. Near, the
garden is full of nothing, as it were summer's ghost haunting
itself. There is no longer any mystery about it. Six weeks ago the
bird-nest was invisible: this morning it stares louder than a
question-mark. Afar, you can see through woods which in
October were opaque. Clean through them you can see—quick as
a whistle—clear to the far side and the second ridge of hills
beyond the far side. Pinned back on the sky, all trees assume
prophetic roles; and above them the stars are symbolic destinations. Tennyson caught the mood:

> Tonight the wind began to rise
> And roar from yonder dripping day;
> The last red leaf is whirled away,
> And rooks are blown about the skies.

The corners of crevices are bare. In September the angle between the woodshed and its door was a lushland of weed, sawdust, ashes, webs; now the wind and rain have rinsed it whiter
than a butcher's table. Cart tracks, too: in March they were
Sargasso Seas; in June, a pillar of dust; today they glow like
mahogany. You can kick them without damaging anything except
your big toe. Streams are bare . . . blue-eyed and bare. No grass
flops into them like a lout's hair. The water is a dull mirror whereon the reeds quiver and are querulous.

In January the sky can become bareness unbared. You might
polish it all day, and still it would seem no smoother. At nightfall
the stars are so bare that you suppose they had never before been
honest with you. Even earth's ornaments are bare. Holly berries,

for instance, show no grime nor moisture. Jessamine is burnished and paler than lemon.

Down by the sea it is the same. The coast is bare . . . no visitors, no fag-ends, and only such ships and birds are as ornaments without decoration. Gales have swept the gulls' droppings from the tarpaulin of a hibernating yacht. Except at high springs, when mud comes down from the creek, the waves seem never so much themselves as in midwinter. You might fancy they had obeyed W. B. Yeats:

> Seek those images
> That constitute the wild. . . .

As with the sea, so at dawn and dusk; all are bare. And they are silent, too. When at last the day does break, no choir comes out to greet it. Through damp half-light the hedgerows twitter thinly; and that is all, unless a cow complains about the lack of central heating, or squirrels rustle to their secret larder. By breakfast-time not even a robin taunts the gloom.

Gilbert White made a curious entry about robins: "The red-breast," he noted, "sings all through the spring, summer and autumn." But robins will carol the new year also, far beyond the twelve days of Christmas. However, the Selborne cleric hailed a countryman's habit of being about in all weathers: "These his pursuits, by keeping the body and mind employed, have, under Providence, contributed to much health and cheerfulness of spirits, even to old age." The men of the Fen district will say Amen to that, for an icy spell still brings out the dyke skaters. Elsewhere—in Derbyshire, Lakeland, and the Scottish hills—a leaden sky raises the hopes of winter-sporters. Older than all of them, beaglers and fox-hunters would not exchange a January day for a week of sun-tanned August.

Persons whose pursuits are less highly specialised tend to feel the cold more keenly, perhaps because they lack a pink coat. In Devon the postmistress blows on her blue knuckles: " 'Tis praper fingery, midear." In Wales a farmer slaps the counter: "Never mind about one for the road, man. Just fill it up with two for me. 'Way up my place there's a foot of snow already. Supper-time I'll be digging-out the sheep, I shouldn't wonder." In the West Riding a dalesman chucks another log on the fire: "Thee mun keep warm, missus." Then he re-reads a belated Christmas greeting from the Inland Revenue: "Happen there's nowt else left in't life." Again he quizzes the questionnaire: "If this gang wins next election, they'll be asking how much Santa Claus put in't bairn's stocking."

January rings the changes on its own rigours. When the mist has cleared, a leafless land looks new because it appears wider. Hillocks become hills; hills tiptoe toward mountains; mountains join the clouds. And through it all—unseen, unsung, illpaid—an army of wintry warriors hack the frozen water-trough, shoulder the life-giving bale, and generally keep an eye on all creatures both great and small. This is a bare season indeed, recalling the Latin playwright's jest about stripping a naked body. It is what we had forgotten in August; what in September became once more a memory; in October, a possibility; in November, probable; in December, inevitable; and now at last a fact.

Coleridge said that all seasons ought to be dear to us. Certainly the months cannot be weighed one against the others. Each is unique and therefore peerless. Yet some people shrink from a bleak midwinter when

> Short-lived sunshine gives no heat,
> Undue buds are nipped by frost,
> Snow sets forth a winding-sheet,
> And all hope of life seems lost.

The men who long ago baptised this month were more patient than Christina Rossetti, for they knew that January was indeed a Janus or custodian of gateways, and that each new year is a threshold of the spring.

Index